ablished
brands,
n travel.

ears our
e secrets
e world,
sharing with travellers a wealth of
experience and a passion for travel.

**Rely on Thomas Cook as your
travelling companion on your next trip
and benefit from our unique heritage.**

Thomas Cook **pocket** guides

VILNIUS

Your travelling companion since 1873

Written by Andrew Quested & Jeroen van Marle, updated by Richard Schofield

Published by Thomas Cook Publishing
A division of Thomas Cook Tour Operations Limited
Company registration no. 3772199 England
The Thomas Cook Business Park, Unit 9, Coningsby Road,
Peterborough PE3 8SB, United Kingdom
Email: books@thomascook.com, Tel: +44 (0) 1733 416477
www.thomascookpublishing.com

Produced by Cambridge Publishing Management Limited
Burr Elm Court, Main Street, Caldecote CB23 7NU
www.cambridgepm.co.uk

ISBN: 978-1-84848-415-3

© 2006, 2008 Thomas Cook Publishing
This third edition © 2011 Thomas Cook Publishing
Text © Thomas Cook Publishing
Maps © Thomas Cook Publishing/PCGraphics (UK) Limited
Transport map © Communicarta Limited

Series Editor: Karen Beaulah
Production/DTP: Steven Collins

Printed and bound in Spain by GraphyCems

Cover photography © Ula Holigrad/Alamy

CONTENTS

SYMBOLS KEY

The following symbols are used throughout this book:

ⓐ address ☎ telephone ⓦ website address ⓔ email
🕒 opening times Ⓝ public transport connections ❶ important

The following symbols are used on the maps:

𝒊	information office	▪	point of interest
✈	airport	○	city
➕	hospital	○	large town
🚌	bus station	○	small town
🚆	railway station	=	motorway
✝	cathedral	—	main road
❶	numbers denote		minor road
	featured cafés & restaurants	—	railway

Hotels and restaurants are graded by approximate price as follows:
£ budget price **££** mid-range price **£££** expensive

◗ *Vilnius's skyline*

INTRODUCING
Vilnius

Introduction

Vilnius, capital of Lithuania, will seduce you in a way that few other cities can. It's a city on a human scale, with an uncanny ability to capture hearts. It doesn't conform to expectations, wriggles free of the confines of any headline and refuses to be slotted into any particular category. But although not many visitors can put their finger on the main attraction, they return time and again. The city's reputation is growing by the day and it's set to become one of the most popular destinations in the Baltic region. Now is the time to visit.

Perhaps, in fact, the appeal lies in Vilnius's lack of a main attraction. There's an architectural and historical tapestry of different styles and stories, sights, sounds and smells, that can't be caught in a single image. But the experience as a whole will gently seep into your senses while you're here and then refuse to leave when you do. Whether you're a backpacker or taking a short break in one of Vilnius's eclectic hotels, you'll find plenty to explore during your visit.

History is raw and recent in Lithuania. Vilnius retains a sense of this, both in its architecture and in the customs of its residents. At one time the capital of a regional superpower, at other times fallen victim to a variety of conquerors, the city's buildings display a mishmash of disparate influences from both East and West. And the architectural landscape is still changing fast, as investment fuelled by EU membership starts to make its mark. Old buildings are being restored and shiny new ones thrown up all over town. Nestled among a confusing array of cobbled streets and an abundance of small churches, the new buildings give you a sense of history still in the making.

Lithuanians are as varied a race as the buildings among which they live. You'll see characters of all sorts either strutting confidently down the street or ambling aimlessly around the alleyways and courtyards. Young, trendy students with all-night party habits intermingle with older residents keen to retain their traditions. Join in with the locals, try their food and favourite drinks and adopt their lifestyle for your visit – you'll learn a whole lot more by doing this than by visiting all the museums in the land.

⬥ The cathedral is one of Vilnius's major attractions

When to go

SEASONS & CLIMATE

June and July are the warmest months, but they are also peak tourist season, so expect higher prices and longer queues. July is also the wettest month of the year and you can find yourself running for cover from a sudden downpour.

The best time to visit Vilnius is spring or autumn – both of which offer explosions of colour, pleasant weather, fewer tourists, and the bustle of a thriving city.

Winters are for the hardy: temperatures occasionally drop below −20°C (−4°F) and days are short and often cloudy. The cold, however, does offer its own appeal. With several layers of clothing you can enjoy crunching the snow in Vilnius's parks, ice-fishing and walking on frozen lakes, or simply listening to the constant warlike rumble of a flowing yet frozen river. Cross-country skiing is also popular with locals.

ANNUAL EVENTS

There is always something going on in Vilnius. Festivals are a mix of pagan and Christian traditions. Catholic calendar highlights including Easter (Velykos) and Shrovetide (Užgavėnės) occur between – or sometimes coincide with – more pagan, nature-inspired events such as the end of winter or Midsummer. You're as likely to see masks, decorations made from twigs and grass and burning wicker people as you are to see crosses, Christian robes and a Nativity scene. The city often erects a stage in Cathedral Square for concerts and celebrations.

Political and historical events are well celebrated, if in a rather haphazard fashion. Advance planning and publicity are not strong

A hot-air balloon drifts past the Gothic St Anne's Church

points. Some details of forthcoming events can be found on the Entertainment Bank website (🅦 www.eb.lt) but it's best to visit the tourist information office as soon as you arrive to find out what's happening.

Apart from Kaziukas Fair in March (see pages 14–15), there are three regular annual events that are definitely worth aiming for.

Užgavėnės (Shrovetide or Fat Tuesday), Tuesday before Ash Wednesday

Shrovetide or Pancake Day, Užgavėnės in Lithuanian, is one of the wildest of Vilnius's annual celebrations. On Shrovetide itself, locals dress head to foot in costumes and impressive masks based on anything from storks to goats to horses. There are mock fights between costumed characters, snowball throwing, singing and chanting – all culminating in the burning of a huge wicker woman. Most of the activities will take place in front of the Town Hall or in Cathedral Square, although you could cop a snowball in the back of the head anywhere.

Joninės (Midsummer), June

This is a good example of a pagan festival that has taken on a Christian meaning. The national holiday, also known as Rasos, Šventė, celebrates the longest day and shortest night of the year. Midsummer Day has been identified as St John's Day, although there's actually nothing Christian about the way it is celebrated here.

Traditionally, girls braid wreaths for themselves from field grass and flowers and then, at midnight, take them off and set them afloat in the river. Girls who are in relationships but are not yet married set two wreaths floating off together. If they stay together, they will marry their beloved, whereas if the wreaths float apart, they will split up. 'He loves me, he loves me not' petal-pinching games are also popular.

◯ *Vilnius gets in the festive spirit at Christmas time*

⬥ *Wearing a floral wreath for Joninės*

Close to midnight a huge fire is lit and rafts are set alight and sent floating down the river. Pick a good spot on a bridge at midnight – the Baltasis Tiltas (White Bridge) is good for this – and take your camera.

If you really want to get involved in the biggest Joninės celebration, head for the town of Kernavė, about 50 km (31 miles) north of Vilnius. Things tend to be very pagan here, and you'll feel like you've travelled back in time as hessian-clad hippies sing, dance, drink mead and set fire to objects around them — all with bird's nests on their heads.

Kernavė Live Archaeology Festival, early July

Kernavė also hosts an annual Live Archaeology Festival, sometimes called Days of Living History. Here you can experience life pretty much as it would have been in ancient times: you can hack pieces off a flame-grilled pig, sit in a tepee made of twigs, try out old-style archery and watch knights in armour battling it out with sticks and maces. The festival normally takes place a couple of weeks after Joninės, in early July. ⓦ www.kernave.org

PUBLIC HOLIDAYS
New Year's Day & National Flag Day 1 Jan
Independence Day 16 Feb
Restoration of Independence Day 11 Mar
Easter Sunday 8 Apr 2012; 31 Mar 2013; 20 April 2014
Workers' Holiday 1 May
Joninės (Midsummer) 20 June 2012; 21 June 2013; 21 June 2014
Crowning of Mindaugas 6 July
Žolinė (Assumption) 15 Aug
All Saints' Day 1 Nov
Christmas Day 25 Dec

Public holidays do not affect visitors to a great extent as most shops and restaurants remain open, except on Christmas Day. Transport runs every day, but weekends and public holidays have a reduced schedule.

Kaziukas Fair

While still dressed in coats of white snow, Vilnius explodes with colour on the first weekend in March as craftspeople flood in from all over the country to sell their wares at Kaziuko Mugė, St Casimir's Fair.

As with many celebrations in Lithuania, the festival's links to Christianity are mingled with an old pagan celebration of the end of winter. St Casimir is the patron saint of Lithuania. He died on 4 March, the time of year when people emerged from hibernation to trade the whittled wooden spoons, woven baskets and dried flower creations they had been working on all winter. March was a good time for travelling and trading, as it was both warm enough to go outside, and cold enough to leave a blanket of snow to drag a sleigh over.

The fair lasts all weekend and, although you don't see too many horses dragging sleighs any more, a good portion of the city is given over to the market. The theme is more or less floral, with *verba* – sticks decorated with dried flowers and grasses from the previous summer – on sale just about everywhere.

In pagan tradition, *verba* had powers of life, health and disease prevention as well as the more practical purpose of making a home smell nicer. Houses were decorated with the colourful floral sticks and people would playfully strike each other on the shoulders and head with them. After Christianity came to Lithuania, *verba* would also be carried to church on Palm Sunday (Verbų Sekmadienis) instead of palm leaves.

You'll also have the opportunity to pick up hand-woven baskets, whittled wooden spoons and other utensils, ironwork, ceramics, and all manner of special, handmade goods. Woodwork and basketwork are particularly popular. Some of the creations you will find on the many stalls are stunning despite their often obscure purpose.

Kaziukas is not only an experience for the colour, hustle and bustle of the market, and the beautiful *verba* that abound. There is also a special feeling of celebration in the air as winter is coming to a close. It's a good example of the mix of pagan and Christian traditions that are now so much a part of Lithuanian culture.

◆ Vilnius takes to the streets for the Kaziukas Fair

History

The region where Lithuania now lies was once covered by a glacier, and when the glacier receded, the first inhabitants to move in were reindeer. Hunting tribes were not far behind them, arriving as early as the 7th century BC. Vilnius itself first came into being in the 11th century when a wooden castle was built on Gediminas Hill to overlook a small settlement below.

Lithuania's first king, Mindaugas, was crowned in 1253 and was responsible for introducing Christianity to Lithuania. He established the cathedral in Vilnius, but the population was not impressed. They accepted the new religion's existence but carried on with their pagan traditions of worshipping the sun, tending fires, dancing in the woods and paying homage to nature.

There followed one of Lithuania's most influential periods in history, when Vilnius found itself at the head of a huge regional superpower stretching southeast as far as the Black Sea. In 1323, Grand Duke Gediminas invited foreigners to settle in Vilnius with the promise of religious freedom, and later formed a union with Poland by marrying his daughter, Aldona, to the son of the then Polish king. These two moves combined to create a strong Lithuanian–Polish kingdom, which flourished and expanded for the next two centuries. Teutonic Knights attacked in 1410 but were defeated in the Battle of Žalgiris, also known as Grunwald.

In the 16th century, however, the Lithuanian–Polish dynasty faltered. Polish became the state language of the region and wars with Russia and Sweden further weakened Lithuania. In 1795, Russia seized Vilnius and all but the most western parts of the country. The Russian occupation lasted 120 years, interrupted only by Napoleon and his army on their ill-fated campaign to Moscow in 1812.

The Russian occupation continued until the Germans arrived to take their place in World War I; independence was finally declared in 1918. Shortly after, Vilnius was seized again by the Poles, who'd been a majority in the city for centuries. Lithuania then managed to remain independent until 1940 when the Soviet Union invaded and, in June 1941, after launching Operation Barbarossa against the Soviets, the Germans captured the city. As a result, almost all Lithuanian Jews were summarily executed by the German regime while hordes of other Lithuanians found themselves being sent off to Siberia under the Soviets. Lithuanian partisans fled to the forest and waged guerrilla-style warfare against the Soviet occupation. The West turned their backs and ignored their pleas for help.

As the Soviet Union started to crumble, Lithuania declared independence again in 1990. The Soviets did not listen, however, and in 1991 Soviet forces attempted to storm the Lithuanian parliament and Vilnius TV Tower. Thirteen unarmed Lithuanian civilians were killed – a tiny number compared to the hundreds of thousands that had died in the previous years – but the event had much greater symbolic significance. This time the world took notice, and before long Soviet statues were being pulled down all over Lithuania.

Steady independence has given Lithuania a springboard for development and the country's future will hopefully be happier than its past. The country reintroduced its own currency, competed under its own flag at the Winter Olympics in 1992 and joined the European Union and NATO in 2004. Since 1 January 2008, it has been a member of the Schengen Agreement.

In 2009 the country celebrated the 1,000th anniversary of the first mention of the word 'Lithuania' in written texts and was also named one of two European Capitals of Culture. In the same year, Dalia Grybauskaitė became the country's first female president.

Lifestyle

Life can be tough for many Lithuanians, but despite this, they certainly know how to have a good time. Theatres and concert halls are regularly packed, and Vilnius's bars and restaurants are almost always buzzing. Lithuanians like to eat, drink and be merry and – contrary to the Russian cliché – enjoy their excellent local beers as much as a shot of vodka.

Vilnius's large student population means that bars and nightclubs are often open all week and tend not to close until as late as 05.00 or 06.00 at weekends. While there are always plenty of places to have a drink in the evening, nightclubs don't fire up until after 23.00. Certainly, Vilnius is a city that seldom sleeps, particularly in summer.

While Vilnius is far from the bargain it once was due to steadily rising prices, it can still be moderately cheap for Western tourists. Living in Lithuania on a local wage is increasingly tough, however, and you should bear this in mind when taxi drivers or restaurant owners try to charge over the odds. Be clear about rates before accepting a ride or booking a service – the tourist information office should be able to give you up-to-date advice on reasonable prices to expect.

Cultural differences are something to be aware of. Lithuanians tend to be reserved and quiet, but are nevertheless friendly once you break the ice. However, concepts of personal space and politeness don't match with those in the West. People tend to queue uncomfortably close to one another to avoid people pushing in, so be prepared for this and don't be afraid to stand your ground. When passing people who are blocking doors or corridors, a quick shove is as normal as a polite 'excuse me' and will often have much more success. Rather than simple rudeness, put this down to local habits – watch what others do and get ready to join in.

◆ *Relaxing by the water's edge*

Culture

Vilnius may be small, but it's packed full of cultural attractions. This is partly because of its rich and complex history. Arts were well funded during Soviet times and standards of education and training in this field were high. As a result, you'll find that theatre, music and dance here are at least as good as in much bigger capitals. The city's location on the crossroads between East and West has also helped. Artists from all corners of the world come to Vilnius, providing a wealth of cultural experiences for visitors.

Performance arts – opera, music, drama – are the main cultural highlights of Vilnius, although there are several worthwhile museums in the city. Be aware, however, that ballet and opera performances are rare during summer, as most locals take their holidays in this period. Museums can also adopt some irregular opening hours.

A good source of information on museums in Vilnius and Lithuania can be found on ⓦ www.muziejai.lt. Most museums and galleries charge a small admission fee, usually under 5Lt.

Before you even think of going to a museum, or to the opera or theatre, keep in mind that there are some fascinating cultural titbits scattered about in the streets. To some extent, Vilnius is a city of secrets. You could be right next to something of note, but not realise until someone points it out or tells you the story behind it. It's also possible to find quaint courtyards or attractive buildings tucked away behind seemingly rundown areas of town.

A guided tour by a knowledgeable local will certainly enhance your cultural experience of the city. The tourist information offices (see page 153) offer regular, good-quality – if a little theatrical – tours. As well as the standard walking tours of the city, you can join in a traditional feast (slice-your-own hog roast using a lettuce leaf as

◔ *Vilnius on a winter's day*

● *Traditional dance performance*

a plate, washed down by medieval mead from a clay tusk) or spend an evening watching and learning traditional dances.

Regular tours generally leave from the cathedral (see pages 62 & 64) at 10.00 and 15.00, but it's best to check times in advance. If you are interested in a particular subject area, such as art, religion, graffiti, ghosts or legends, ask at the tourist information offices about hiring a private guide.

◗ *The river winding its way through the city*

MAKING THE MOST OF
Vilnius

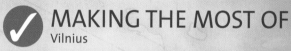

Shopping

Vilnius is not a shopping destination or even, nowadays, a hive of bargains. Shopping here is definitely, however, a worthwhile experience, particularly in the old-fashioned markets and the snakeskin-boots-'n-bling shops.

One of the most fun markets is perched on the top of Tauras Hill, in and around the Trade Union Palace. On Saturday mornings, the area is filled with stalls offering military memorabilia, collectables including stamps, badges and coins, and assorted antiques that could make interesting souvenirs.

You'll find a handful of these sellers and more at the eastern edge of the mainstream Kalvarijų Market (see page 98), held just outside of the centre every morning except Monday. You may be able to seek out a bargain from the collection of items for sale –

AMBER – OR TOFFEE?

When buying amber, take special care that you are buying the genuine product. Mosaics made of hundreds of little chips of 'amber' have been known to melt and dribble down the wall when hung in direct sunlight – because, in fact, they're not made of amber at all but of toffee. You can test amber by sniffing or tasting it (it shouldn't be sweet or plasticky) or by burning it (real amber, when burnt, smells like pine-scented air freshener). Most sellers will object to your trying either method. Sugar can be discreetly spotted with a damp finger, but a good guide is the price – you get what you pay for. Try to buy from reputable amber shops rather than street-side stalls.

⬥ Shopping in Vilnius has changed dramatically since Soviet days

anything from goldfish to second-hand boots to electronics and fake brand names. Whatever you buy, you can carry it with dignity by giving one of the old lady sellers a few coins in return for a plastic shopping bag from an expensive fashion store.

Near the train station is the bustling **Halės Market** (❸ Pylimo & Bazilijonų ◐ Early–13.00 daily) selling all manner of produce, from meat and honey to imported clothing. It's a fascinating experience for the gourmand as well as an eye-opener for anyone used to supermarkets. If you do want a supermarket, look out for Iki, Maxima and Rimi stores dotted about the city. Rimi is the higher-quality option, selling a good range of otherwise hard-to-find goods.

⬤ *Market day in Gedimino Avenue*

USEFUL SHOPPING PHRASES

What time do the shops open/close?
Kada atidaromos uždaromos/parduotuvės?
Kah-dah ah-teeh-dah-roh-mohs uzh-darr-om-oss/
pahr-dot-oov-ess?

How much is this?
Kiek šitas kainuoja?
Keck sheetus kay-noh-ya?

Can I try this on?
Ar galima pasimatuoti?
Ur gull-im-uh pass-im-ah-totee?

My size is ...
Mano dydis ...
Mah-noh dee-diss ...

I'll take this one, thank you
Aš šitą paimsiu, ačiū
Ash sheet-ah pah-im-soo, ah-choo

This is too large/too small/too expensive. Do you have any others?
Per didelis/per mažas/per brangus. Ah turite kà kitų?
Perr did-el-iss/perr mazh-us/perr bran-goose. Ah toor-it-teh
kah ki-too?

There are several modern shopping centres to satisfy your retail needs. Gedimino Avenue is the main drag, with some interesting shops tucked all the way down the western end. The most recent addition, Vilniaus Vartai, or 'Gates of Vilnius', features the latest flurry of designer shops. Europa (see page 98) is modern but fairly small and predictable. For a larger choice of stores, try Akropolis (see page 96), which has an ice rink in the centre, or the recently opened Panorama (see page 99).

Eating & drinking

Lithuanians traditionally like real hearty man-food: meat and potatoes. Local food is simple but fresh and tasty, and generally of good value. A typical lunchtime meal is battered or fried meat such as pork or chicken, boiled potatoes, and a 'white salad' of more potatoes, peas and carrots in mayonnaise. A local version of coleslaw is often served as an accompaniment.

The unofficial Lithuanian national dish is *cepelinai*, or 'zeppelins'. Originating in Germany, *cepelinai* are round dumplings made of grated potato wrapped around a piece of spiced meat or curd. They are normally served with a sauce, and the type of sauce reflects the different regional variations of the dish.

Vederai are another traditional variation on the theme of meat and potatoes, consisting of a grilled sheep's intestine filled with creamy mashed potato. Think of it as a potato sausage, as it tastes a lot better than it sounds. You'll find these dishes on offer in many restaurants and they tend to be the best-value option. They're certainly a good way of keeping warm in cold weather. International food is also widely available and of generally good quality, but tends to be more expensive than the local favourites.

Lithuanians enjoy a drink, particularly beer, and will proudly remind you that the local brews often win medals and accolades

PRICE CATEGORIES
Based on the average price of a three-course meal without drinks.
£ up to 15Lt   ££ 15–25Lt   £££ over 25Lt

⬥ *Friendly faces and tasty beer all around*

USEFUL DINING PHRASES

I would like a table for ... people
Norėčiau staliuko ... žmonėms
Norr-etch-ow stah-lyoo-koh ... zhmo-nems

May I have the bill, please?
Ar galite atnešti sàskaità?
Ur gull-i-teh at-nesh-tee sass-kay-tah?

Waiter/Waitress!
Padavėjau/Padavėja!
Pah-dah-veh-yau/ Pah-dah-veh-yah!

Could I have it well-cooked/medium/rare, please?
Ah galite iškepti visiškai/vidutiniškai/su krauju?
Ur gull-i-teh ish-kept-ee wee-seesh-kay/wee-doo-teenie-shkay/soo crow-yoo?

I am a vegetarian. Does this contain meat?
Aš vegetaras. Ar tai su mėsa?
Ash veh-geh-tah-rahs. Ahr tay suh meh-sah?

Where is the toilet, please?
Kur tualetas?
Coor too-al-ett-us?

I would like a cup of/two cups of/another coffee/tea
Prašom puodel/du puodelius/dar kavos/arbatos
Pras-shom poh-deh-lee/doo poh-deh-loos/dahr kah-voss/ ar-bat-oss

in international competitions. The beer tends to be light, crisp, and easy to drink. Be wary, though, as although the beer may look light, its alcoholic content is not. Soak it up with some *užkandžiai prie alaus*, popular beer snacks including *kepta duona*, little sticks of fried dark bread covered with melted cheese or garlic. For the more adventurous, there are pigs' ears.

In both restaurants and bars, tipping is not required but is a reward for good service. Rounding up your bill to avoid small change or offering an extra ten per cent or so is standard.

Smoking is not permitted in any restaurants, cafés, bars, clubs or other public places. There are one or two places that have a special smoking room, but these are rare.

The whole restaurant scene takes on a different atmosphere in summer, when dozens of outdoor cafés and eateries appear, seemingly from nowhere, and fill streets and courtyards alike. Each of these is attached to a bricks-and-mortar venue, although it can be hard to tell which belongs to which. It's very relaxing to sit outside with a beer or coffee, people-watching until the late evening in summer.

Picnicking is not common among Lithuanians but there's nothing to stop you stocking up at a food market or supermarket (see page 26) and heading for a local park or bench. Locals tend to eat alfresco only out of town, setting up barbecues for friends and family around one of the country's many lakes.

Entertainment & nightlife

One of the great joys of Vilnius is the quality and variety of performances that you can see without making a dent in your holiday budget. Lithuanians, despite what you may think from the Eurovision Song Contest, place a strong emphasis on music and theatre and are proud to show off the excellent results.

In addition, touring artists often turn up in Vilnius and you can sometimes catch big-name international acts without the astronomical ticket prices that you would pay at home. Older heavy metal and rock acts often appear here and the arena in which they play is jokingly called the 'graveyard'.

Theatre is varied and always of good quality, but is generally only performed in Lithuanian. Despite this, the creativity and energy can still make this a moving experience.

For information on upcoming performances, see ⓦ www.eb.lt. Tickets can generally be purchased at the venue on the evening of the performance, or booked in advance via the theatre's website. There is also a ticket booth in the public square opposite the Novotel hotel on Gedimino Avenue.

In warmer months – May to August – you can also come across excellent free music and dance in public spaces. Keep an eye on Cathedral Square, Town Hall Square and the larger Old Town courtyards, especially on public holidays and festival days. Chances are you'll come across some traditional Lithuanian performances, which can be a real treat. If you happen to be in town in the week before Christmas, you'll find many churches put on free, atmospheric concerts.

A more recent Lithuanian tradition is clubbing until dawn, in one of Vilnius's many eclectic late-night bars and nightclubs.

If you're going out on the town for a spot of late-night dancing, a favourite pastime of young Lithuanians, note that admission to some nightclubs can be as high as 60Lt depending on the venue and night.

◆ *There's a wide choice of bars and clubs*

Sport & relaxation

SPECTATOR SPORTS

Basketball is like a second religion in Lithuania. The Vilnius team is Lietuvos Rytas, and a game between them and their sworn rivals Žalgiris (from Kaunas) is the Lithuanian equivalent of Real Madrid versus FC Barcelona in Spain. Indeed, it's such an event that Lithuania's borders have been known to close when a game this big is on. See Ⓦ www.lkl.lt for local league information.

The biggest games are played at **Siemens Arena** (ⓐ Ozo 14 ⓣ 5247 7576 Ⓜ Bus: 53, 62 to Pramogų Arena). For information on games and to book online, see Ⓦ www.bilietai.lt. Schedules and tickets are also available from **Tiketa** (Ⓦ www.tiketa.lt).

Even if you can't make it to a game, watching it live in any bar or club in Vilnius is also a great experience – especially if the Vilnius team wins. Be careful not to antagonise any locals if they don't win, however, as there have been reports of some nasty scenes during the European Basketball Championships and other major international competitions in which Lithuania competes.

Football is also played, but is by no measure as popular as basketball.

PARTICIPATION SPORTS

Lithuania is a land of lakes and rivers, so canoeing and kayaking are popular. You can even combine this with camping for a pleasant and quite unique holiday. It's best to go through a specialised tour agency such as **Active Holidays** (Ⓦ www.activeholidays.lt).

RELAXATION

A pampering must is a sauna and spa. Most good hotels in town have their own facilities that can be booked by the hour, usually at a special rate for guests. Three of the best are at the Amberton hotel (see page 39), Radisson Blu Astorija (see page 40) and Narutis (see page 39).

Another option is to head out of town to a sauna and spa in a village, which can be delightful, especially in winter when you can combine it with jumping about in the snow or plunging through a hole in a frozen lake. You can add local flavour by asking to be whacked by a leafy birch branch (*vanotis vantom*) or by requesting a honey massage (*masažas su medum*). Ask one of the tourist information offices to recommend a spa that is currently active in Trakai or Molėtai. If you want to stay overnight, head over to Druskininkai (see pages 112–21).

Be sure when you are booking a sauna that it is clear exactly what you want. If you are quoted what seems like an exorbitantly high price, you are probably being offered 'company', not just the use of the sauna.

● *Basketball is enjoyed by Lithuanians of all ages*

Accommodation

There is a good range of hotels in Vilnius, covering everything from cheap hostels to luxury five-star hotels. There are certainly hotels that lay on the luxury and offer a good-value treat, but there are also more cosy affairs that have plenty of charm without the high prices. Self-catering apartments and B&B-style accommodation are also available, offering excellent value if you prefer to be a bit more independent. Budget travellers can choose from a small selection of basic hostels with, generally, a fun and friendly atmosphere.

The bigger hotels accept bookings online, while some of the smaller places, including apartments and B&Bs, will accept email enquiries and faxes. Out of the summer season, you can often find accommodation just by turning up without a reservation, but with Vilnius's growing popularity it's always best to book.

HOTELS

Shakespeare Boutique ££ Vilnius's best-known boutique hotel, tucked away in a quiet backstreet but near Cathedral Square. Rooms are themed on famous authors and literary characters. The unique décor and friendliness of the staff offer a home-away-from-home atmosphere. ❸ Bernardinų 8/8 ❶ 5266 5885 Ⓦ www.shakespeare.lt Ⓝ Bus: 10, 11, 33 to Daliės Akademija

> **PRICE CATEGORIES**
> Based on the average price of a double room for one night.
> **£** up to 150Lt   **££** 150–400Lt   **£££** over 400Lt

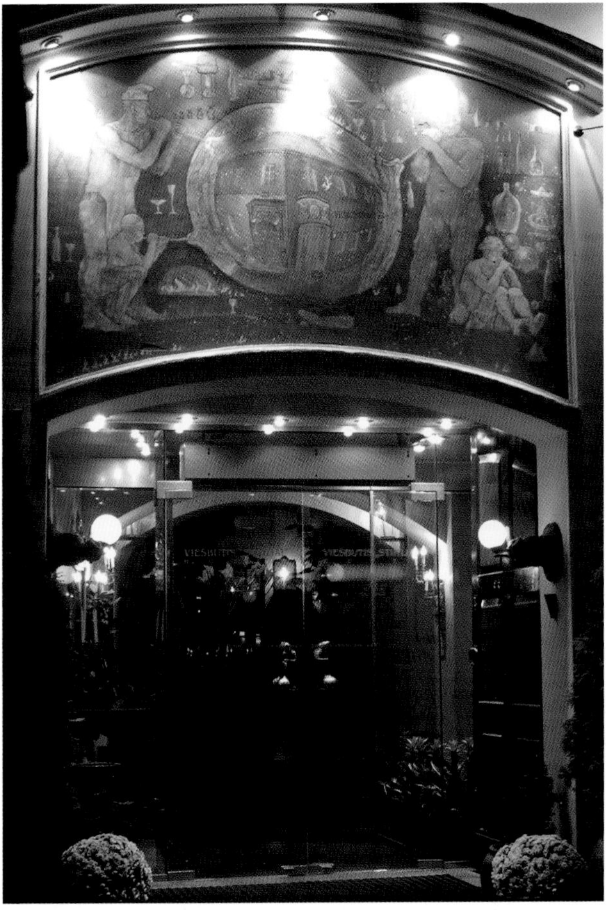

The Stikliai hotel is one of the most refined in Vilnius

Some of the best rooms in Vilnius are in the Novotel

Amberton £££ On the corner of Cathedral Square, this large but homely hotel has one of the widest range of facilities and room choices around. Don't miss the spa and sauna facilities hidden away downstairs. ⓐ Stuokos-Gucevičiaus 3 ❶ 5210 7461 ⓦ www.ambertonhotels.com ⓝ Bus: 33 to Arkikatedra; 11 to Gedimino

Atrium £££ The Atrium offers large rooms, clean and simple yet with all the luxuries you want, including leather furniture, wireless phones and large-screen televisions. The location near Castle Hill and the cathedral is excellent, as is the Argentinian-style steak restaurant. ⓐ Pilies 10 ❶ 5210 7777 ⓦ www.atrium.lt ⓝ Bus: 10, 11, 33 to Sereikiškių

Europa Royale Vilnius £££ An ostentatious and opulent hideaway decorated by Italian designers. The standard rooms are more subdued but in any case service is excellent. ⓐ Aušros Vartų 6 ❶ 5266 0770 ⓦ www.groupeuropa.com ⓝ Bus: 4, 11, 13, 31, 34, 74; trolleybus: 1, 2, 5, 7 to Rūdninkų

Narutis £££ You're really getting something special here, and not just due to the outstanding location. Rooms have all been individually decorated by a French designer, with frescoes and original elements of the 16th-century building exposed. ⓐ Pilies 24 ❶ 5212 2894 ⓦ www.narutis.com ⓝ Bus: 10, 11, 33 to Sereikiškių

Novotel £££ One of the least attractive buildings in the Old Town but with some of the finest rooms, many with great views. Décor is fairly minimalist, but both the hotel and the rooms have everything you need including free Wi-Fi. One room is set aside for guests with

disabilities. Gedimino 16 5266 6200 www.novotel.com Bus: 26, 43, 53; trolleybus: 2, 3, 5, 6, 12, 14 to Vilniaus

Radisson Blu Astorija £££ Charming building with rather strict, square but comfortable and clean rooms. The location right behind the Town Hall is excellent. George W Bush once stayed here. Free Wi-Fi. Didžioji 35/2 5212 0110 www.radissonblu.com Bus: 4, 11, 13, 31, 34, 74; trolleybus: 1, 2, 5, 7 to Rūdninkų

Ramada £££ Italian-style décor with a modern twist – gilded furniture, marble-topped tables and flat-screen televisions and DVD players in all rooms. Free Wi-Fi or LAN Internet access. Subačiaus 2 5255 3355 www.ramadavilnius.lt Bus: 4, 11, 13, 31, 34, 74; trolleybus: 1, 2, 5, 7 to Rūdninkų

Stikliai £££ Near the university and exquisite in every respect, with a very refined but charming Mediterranean feel. It's a hotel you stay in to impress and a favourite with visiting VIPs. Gaono 7 5264 9595 www.stikliaihotel.lt Bus: 11 to Vokiečių

APARTMENTS & B&Bs

Litinterp £–££ This long-standing, reputable B&B booking service is the best way to find basic, comfortable accommodation without denting your budget. They also offer home-stay accommodation and a range of other travel services. Bernardinų 7/2 5212 3850 www.litinterp.com Bus: 10, 11, 33 to Dalies Akademija

Avenue Apartments ££ Two fine apartments on the city's main shopping street close to several sights. Facilities include satellite television, fully equipped kitchens and en-suite bathroom facilities.

ⓐ Gedimino 44/3 ❶ 6701 9627 ⓦ www.vilnius-apartment.com
Ⓝ Bus: 2, 23; trolleybus: 4, 11, 13, 17

HOSTELS

A Hostel £ Not just one, but a whole cluster of new and funky hostels, one of which features Japanese-style bed pods. All locations are centred around Stepono and within easy walking distance of both the Old Town and the bus and train stations. ⓐ Sodų 17 ❶ 5215 0270 ⓦ www.ahostel.lt

Filaretai £ The furthest away from all the Old Town action, the Filaretai is located in the alternative Užupis district (see pages 82–91). Walking to or from this hostel is half the fun, except if you're alone and it's very late at night. It is part of the IYH network and also has bicycles available for hire. ⓐ Filaretų 17 ❶ 5215 4627 ⓦ www.filaretai hostel.lt Ⓝ Bus: 27, 34, 37, 44 to Filaretų

Old Town Hostel £ A small, comfortable, friendly and well-run hostel, conveniently located within easy walking distance of the bus and train stations. Free Wi-Fi. ⓐ Aušros Vartų 20/15 ❶ 5262 5357 ⓦ www.oldtownhostel.lt

THE BEST OF VILNIUS

Getting the most out of Vilnius requires an open mind, a desire to explore, a pair of feet and the willingness to use them. Often the best things are somewhat hidden in a tucked-away courtyard or behind a door that may not look too inviting. Do be inquisitive, and don't be shy.

TOP 10 ATTRACTIONS

- **St Anne's Church** The architectural gem of Vilnius (see pages 68–9).

- **Cathedral** Book a tour of the cellars to really delve into the city's history (see pages 62 & 64).

- **KGB Museum (Museum of Genocide Victims)** Stoic, disconcerting and even a bit sickening – but a mind-opening experience (see pages 67–8).

- **Higher Castle Museum (Gedimino Pilis)** Catch the magnificent view from the top (see page 70).

- **Applied Arts Museum** Nearly all of Vilnius's arty treasures are tucked away in here (see page 70).

- **The Old Town** Charming streets, quirky courtyards, inviting cafés and a myriad of ways to get lost (see pages 62–81).

- **Dinner in a cellar** Burrow into Lokys (see pages 76–7) or Žemaičiai (see page 77) for traditional *cepelinai* (see page 28) in a cellar.

- **Markets** A trip to a market can be like a jaunt in a time machine – and they'll try to sell you anything (see pages 24, 26 & 98).

- **Užupis** A trendy and alternative area, a self-designated breakaway independent republic (see pages 82–91). Look for the constitution on the wall along Paupio Gatvė (see page 85).

- **Dawn Gate** The original 16th-century gates to the city, shielding a glowing image of the Virgin Mary (see page 64).

🔽 *A Renaissance façade in the Old Town*

Suggested itineraries

HALF-DAY: VILNIUS IN A HURRY

When you're pushed for time, concentrate on the area around the cathedral (see pages 62 & 64). Here you can visit the Higher Castle Museum (Gedimino Pilis, see page 70), the Applied Arts Museum (see page 70) and of course the cathedral itself. Finish off by wandering down Pilies Street to the Town Hall and back, and stop off for a quick lunch or coffee at any of the many street-side cafés.

1 DAY: TIME TO SEE A LITTLE MORE

With a little more time, you can explore the Old Town (see pages 62–81) more fully – and that simply means walking. Head in pretty much any direction from the Town Hall and you'll find yourself in a network of charming streets. The mixture of charming and crumbling delights you will come across is fascinating. For Jewish history and culture, head south towards Geto Aukų Aikštė (Ghetto Victims' Square) and keep your eyes peeled for plaques with Yiddish inscriptions along the way.

2–3 DAYS: TIME TO SEE MUCH MORE

Squeezing in a trip to Trakai (see pages 102–11) is a must. The town is home to a Gothic castle nestled on an island in a lake, with attractive greenery on all the surrounding banks.

LONGER: ENJOYING VILNIUS TO THE FULL

In summer, exploring Lithuania's fantastic national parks and lakes is sublime. If you can, take a trip to the unique UNESCO World Heritage Site of the Curonian Spit (see pages 124–5). The Hill of Crosses in Šiauliai (see page 125) should be on your list too. Both are

🔺 *Higher Castle is an icon of Vilnius*

a fair distance from Vilnius and really deserve an overnight stay to do them justice. Closer by are Kernavė (see pages 12–13) and Molėtai, the former boasting some interesting history and the latter an area of gorgeous lakes.

If you still have a day to spare after this, jump on a bus to Grūto Parkas near Druskininkai, a theme park filled with Lithuania's old Soviet statues of Lenin and Stalin (see pages 114–17).

Something for nothing

The best way to enjoy Vilnius without spending a cent – or a *centas* in the local language – is to walk. Exploring the Old Town is a rewarding experience, especially if you deviate from the obvious routes and burrow into little side streets and courtyards. Slip through what may look like a private doorway, and you can discover a whole new side of the city, where one courtyard adjoins another, and then another, before leading to yet another street.

On Vokiečių Street next door to the Žemaičiai restaurant, for example, is a little doorway leading to a courtyard that, with parked cars and the back doors of restaurants, is hardly much of a discovery. At the back of this, however, is a little tunnel – you'll have to crouch to get through it – leading to another courtyard that is well worth discovering. It's a pleasant snapshot of a different way of life. Wooden balconies overlook the yard where locals sometimes sit and chat. A row of wooden storage sheds lines the other side. You've probably only walked 50 m (164 ft), but you'll feel a million miles away from the hustle and bustle of Vokiečių Street.

Another courtyard, on Rūdninkų Street near the corner of Pylimo, boasts an almost intact portion of the otherwise long-gone original city wall.

The routes through these courtyards are not marked on any map as they are actually private property. Keep this in mind as you explore; keep quiet and don't invade the residents' privacy by looking through their windows, and nobody will mind.

Large open public spaces are also worth hanging around in, especially Cathedral Square, Gedimino Avenue and Rotušės (Town Hall) Square. On public holidays and celebrations, there are often markets and fairs where you can try traditional foods as well as see locals dressed in costumes and dancing. Cathedral Square hosts regular free concerts and celebrations on holidays – ask at the tourist information office if there is anything going on.

If you're in Vilnius on April Fools' Day, you'd be a fool not to head to Užupis (see pages 82–91), the self-declared independent republic breakaway district. They'll be happy to stamp your passport and toss you into the midst of all sorts of wacky revelry on that day.

● *Admire the ornate interiors of the Orthodox churches*

When it rains

There's a whole other side of Vilnius to explore when the skies open up – the city's underside. Vilnius is riddled with cellars and crypts. Most have been turned into cafés, bars and nightclubs that play on the cave-like appeal of their location. Others are museums, and others are just plain creepy. Burrowing into such places is an excellent option in bad weather.

The most obvious underground attraction is the network of crypts and rooms beneath the main cathedral (see pages 62 & 64). Reasonably priced tours covering architectural, artistic and political history can be organised at the small shop located in the side of the cathedral. If you have trouble with the language, ask at the tourist information office. Regular tours leave at specified times, or, if there are several of you, consider hiring a private guide for your group.

Several other churches in the city have crypts that can be visited, many of them complete with plenty of graves and tombs. One other related underground experience can be found at the recently opened Tuskulėnai Peace Park Memorial Complex (🅐 Žirmunu 1f 🕐 5275 0704 ❶ Entrance by appointment only), whose haunting subterranean Columbarium houses the remains of over 700 Lithuanians and Poles executed by the KGB between 1944 and 1947 who were found on the site after independence.

If you prefer your history above ground, try the varied and rewarding Higher Castle Museum (Gedimino Pilis, see page 70). Old coins, pieces of uniform from Napoleon's troops and a wide variety of other artefacts have been dug up and presented here, along with informative descriptions in English.

◆ *Discover the crypts beneath the cathedral*

On arrival

TIME DIFFERENCE

Lithuania is two hours ahead of Greenwich Mean Time. Clocks
go forward one hour in March for daylight saving and are turned
back again in October.

ARRIVING

By air

Even with a relatively new terminal and more renovations still under
way, **Vilnius Airport** (☏ 5273 9305 Ⓦ www.vilnius-airport.lt) is a small
and uncomplicated facility. It has a bureau de change and ATM
machine, car-rental desks, a restaurant and café and a useful kiosk
selling phonecards and tickets for public transport.

The Old Town is just 8 km (5 miles) away from the airport and
should take 15 minutes in a taxi. Official rates per kilometre are
written on a sign near the taxi rank outside and you should always
agree on a price before setting off. The standard price is around
40–50Lt but many drivers may try to charge you more, particularly
if it is late or at the weekend.

A cheaper alternative is to take bus 1 or 2 from the stop just
to the left of the arrivals hall. Between three and five buses
leave every hour between 05.00 and 23.00 on weekdays and
between 06.00 and 23.00 at weekends. Tickets can be bought
from the driver.

Ryanair flights arrive at **Kaunas Airport** (☏ 5210 4304 Ⓦ www.
kaunas-airport.lt), around one and a half hours from Vilnius by road.
Private minibuses to the centre, timed to coincide with flight arrivals,
cost 45Lt or 35Lt if you book in advance online (☏ 6724 5400
Ⓦ www.airport-express.lt).

⬤ *Vilnius in spring is vibrant and lush*

You may also like to stop for a while in Kaunas – Lithuania's second-largest city – before you head on to Vilnius. Bus 29 goes from the airport to Kaunas main bus and train stations, from where there are regular connections to Vilnius. On weekdays, there

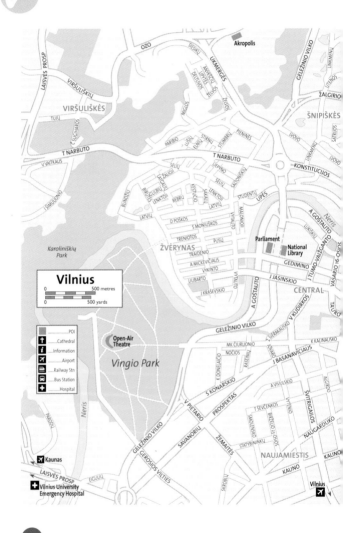

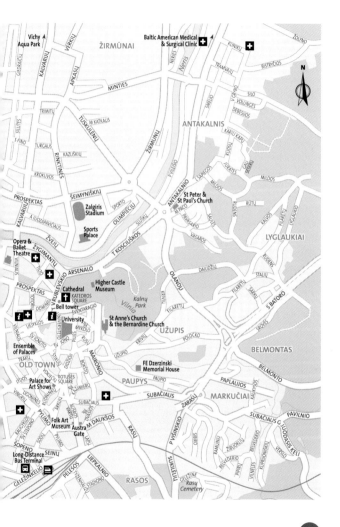

are a few buses every hour from around 05.00 until a little after 22.00. At weekends, buses are less frequent and run from around 06.30 until about 22.00.

By rail

Vilnius railway station (🚉 Geležinkelio 16 📞 5233 0088) is located within walking distance of the Old Town. If you are arriving on an international train, you will have to pass through customs. There is a small kiosk at the station, as well as ATMs and a bureau de change. See 🌐 www.litrail.lt for timetable information.

Opposite the railway station exit is McDonald's – walk past this and carry on down the gentle slope until you come to a four-way intersection with a rail bridge to the right. Turn left here and walk straight ahead. You'll soon pass through the Dawn Gate into the Old Town.

If you don't want to walk, take bus 26, trolleybus 1, 2, 5 or 7, or minibus 1, 2, 4, 5, 7 or 62 straight to the city centre. Taxis are plentiful and should cost around 10Lt to a central hotel.

By road

The main bus station is fairly near the railway station – walk through the station building and once outside, veer to the right. See above for directions on getting to the Old Town from here.

Inside the building, you will find facilities for left luggage, and offices for international bus companies including Eurolines, kiosks, cafés and ATMs.

FINDING YOUR FEET

Vilnius is a relatively small and calm city, although there is always plenty going on – especially in summer. It's the ideal city

IF YOU GET LOST, TRY ...

Excuse me, do you speak English?
Atsiprašau, jūs kalbate angliškai?
Aht-see-prah-show, yoos kahl-bah-teh angle-ish-kay?

Excuse me, is this the right way to ... the cathedral/the tourist office/the castle/the Old Town?
Atsiprašau, ar aš teisingai einu į ... katedrą/turistų biurą/pilį/senamiestį?
Aht-see-prah-show, ur ash tey-sing-ay ay-noo ee ... cutt-ed-rah/too-riss-too byoo-rah/peeli/seh-nah-myes-tee?

Can you point to it on my map?
Ar galite parodyti žemėlapyje?
Ur gull-it-teh purr-oddity zhe-mell-uppie-ya?

for strolling, but be careful on narrow streets, where pedestrians often spill on to the road, and the road seems to be used as a racetrack by cars, taxis and motorbikes.

It is generally a very safe place to visit, but take common-sense precautions by keeping valuables locked in your hotel safe and by not antagonising locals, especially at night.

Beggars can be a problem as they tend to be persistent. The tourist information office has advised visitors not to offer money as there are soup kitchens and charitable organisations in the city which provide beggars with more reliable support. Be firm, refuse loudly and then, if they persist, simply ignore them.

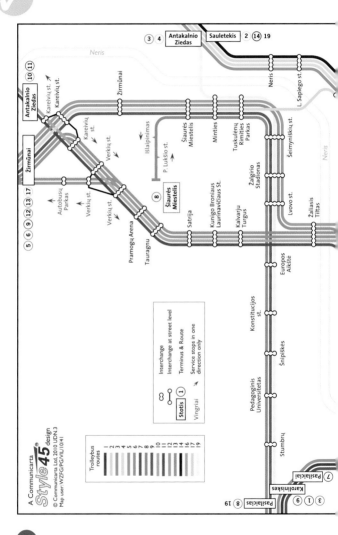

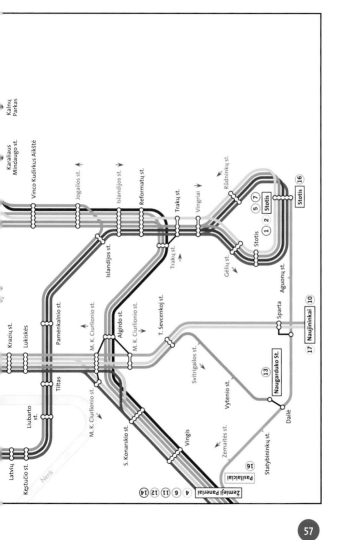

ORIENTATION

Vilnius sprawls out from around the cathedral – a place where two rivers meet in a gentle valley. A tributary of the smaller River Vilnia once flowed along what is now the road leading from the cathedral, Šventaragio. The area of the cathedral is a good orientation point. If you're lost, just say the word 'cathedral' to a passer-by to be pointed in the right direction.

The main attractions lie in an area the shape of a generous pie-wedge, with the cathedral at the point. One edge is the rough line between Pilies, Didžioji and Aušros Vartų streets and the area immediately east of this. The other edge runs along Gedimino Avenue.

◔ An easy way to get around

The streets of Vilnius, with the exception of the long and straight Gedimino Avenue, are confusingly higgledy-piggledy. If your sense of direction is even slightly less than high-grade military GPS standard, don't go too far without a map until you get to know at least the main streets.

GETTING AROUND

Vilnius is small and compact and the best way to get around is by foot. For the few instances when something is too far away to stroll to, Vilnius's comprehensive network of trolleybuses, microbuses and ordinary buses will get you there quickly and cheaply. For comfort's sake, avoid rush hour.

Electric trolleybuses have antennae attached to cables above the road. They are most useful for the inner city centre and their routes and route numbers are marked in red on the city's transport map. Regular diesel buses tend to travel a little further into the outskirts and their routes are marked in blue. Be aware that a trolleybus and regular bus can have the same number but go to completely different destinations. The transport map on pages 56–7 of this guide shows only trolleybuses.

The same tickets can be used for both trolleybuses and regular buses and can be purchased from kiosks marked 'Lietuvos Spauda' or from the driver for a slightly higher rate. Each ticket is valid for a single journey on a single vehicle, and must be validated in either the electronic or the older red 'crimping' devices on board.

Microbuses are licensed, commercially run, and terribly convenient. They are minibuses that tear along numbered routes, picking up and dropping off passengers as required along the way. When you see one coming, put your hand in the air to hail it. The standard rate is 3Lt for a journey, paid to the driver when you get in. Look out for your destination and as you approach make it clear that you want to get off.

Taxis are an inexact science in Vilnius and drivers can be unhelpful, sometimes charging over the odds or refusing to use their meter. A trip within the Old Town in normal hours shouldn't cost more than 20Lt. Booking a taxi in advance is actually cheaper than hailing one in the street. Some taxi firms are:

Martono (ⓣ 5240 0004), **Vilniaus Taksi Plius** (ⓣ 5261 6161), **Ekipažas** (ⓣ 5239 5539) and **Mersera** (ⓣ 5278 8888).

Car hire

The bus network and your own feet will work well enough for exploring the centre of Vilnius, but hiring a car will give you more freedom if you're planning to travel elsewhere. Navigating is easy as there are excellent road signs, but beware some rather haphazard driving from locals in the city centre. When you're on the open road, keep an eye out to avoid horses and carts or slow-moving agricultural machinery.

Most international car-rental companies operate in Lithuania but local options can be cheaper.

Avis ⓐ Rodūnios Kelias 2 (Airport) ⓣ 5232 9316 ⓦ www.avis.lt

Budget ⓐ Rodūnios Kelias 2 (Airport) ⓣ 5230 6708 (24 hrs) ⓦ www.budget.lt

Europcar ⓐ Stuokos-Gucevičiaus 9/1 ⓣ 6863 2971 ⓦ www.europcar.lt

Hertz ⓐ Kalvarijų 14 ⓣ 5272 6940 ⓦ www.hertz.lt

Rimas Rentacar ⓣ 6982 1662 ⓔ rimas.cars@is.lt

Sixt ⓐ Rodūnios Kelias 2 (Airport) ⓣ 5239 5636 ⓦ www.sixt.com

◑ *St Peter and St Paul's Church*

THE CITY OF
Vilnius

Old Town

It won't take you long to see why UNESCO has listed Vilnius Old Town as a World Heritage Site. While that credential doesn't make it unique, the range of architecture on display in Vilnius does. Vilnius has a few hidden architectural treasures that easily rank among the best of their kind in Europe and possibly the world.

Much of Vilnius was shaped by the fact that many different religions and cultures were welcomed here. It was a city of tolerance and acceptance, and the wide range of immigrants all made their particular mark. At the same time, Lithuanians also eloquently expressed their culture in the built environment and the results of this combination are what you see today.

The Old Town is compact enough to get around on foot and this is by far the simplest way to navigate. If you do need to use public transport, obtain a detailed transport map from the tourist information office and check with locals and drivers exactly which buses are going to your destination.

SIGHTS & ATTRACTIONS

Cathedral

The first cathedral on this site was erected in 1251, funded by Grand Duke Mindaugas. There were pagan temples here prior to that, evidence of which is still visible if you take a tour of the cellars (see page 48).

The current building was designed and built by Stuoka-Gucevičius in 1769–1820. The same architect was also responsible for parts of the Presidential Palace and you can see a statue of his stylised head in the little park at the end of the street which bears his name.

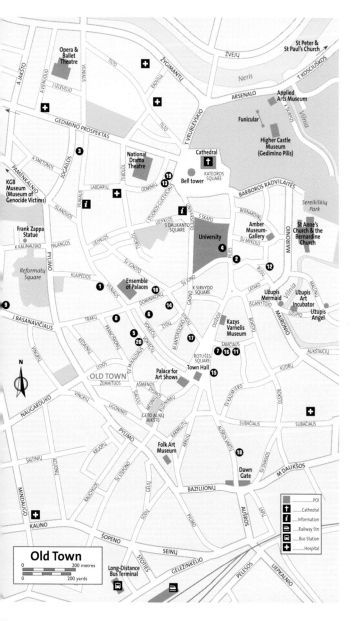

Old Town

0	200 metres
0	200 yards

St Peter & St Paul's Church

Neris

Opera & Ballet Theatre

Applied Arts Museum

Funicular

Higher Castle Museum (Gedimino Pilis)

GEDIMINO PROSPEKTAS

National Drama Theatre

Cathedral

KATEDROS SQUARE

Bell tower

KGB Museum (Museum of Genocide Victims)

Frank Zappa Statue

Reformatų Square

Sereikiškių Park

Amber Museum-Gallery

St Anne's Church & the Bernardine Church

University

Ensemble of Palaces

Užupis Mermaid

Užupis Art Incubator

Užupis Angel

Kazys Varnelis Museum

Palace for Art Shows

ROTUŠĖS SQUARE

Town Hall

OLD TOWN

Folk Art Museum

Dawn Gate

Long-Distance Bus Terminal

Legend:
- POI
- ✝ Cathedral
- i Information
- Railway Stn
- Bus Station
- ✚ Hospital

N

THREE-HANDED SAINT

When you go and visit the cathedral, make sure to stop at the chapel of St Casimir. Look closely at his image in there and you'll see that, apparently, he had three hands. Legend has it that the artist who created the picture decided to change the position of the hand, so he painted over it and drew a new one. The old hand, however, kept reappearing each time it was painted over. The painter eventually concluded that it must be a miracle and left the picture tri-handed.

The cathedral is home to a range of stunning chapels including, in the northeast corner, that of Lithuania's patron saint, Casimir. ⓐ Katedros Square 🕐 08.00–19.00 daily

Dawn Gate

The Dawn Gate was one of the original gates to the city. Visitors had to pay to enter with a rock or stone, thereby contributing directly to the paved streets of the walled city. A chapel was built into the structure above the arched entranceway in 1671 and became home to a glowing image of the Virgin Mary. It is visible through an open window and is believed to have miraculous powers, which is why older locals, mostly women, still kneel in the street before it.

To really appreciate this cornerstone of Vilnius, duck into a little doorway on your left as you are facing the Virgin Mary, climb the stairs and marvel at the neoclassical interior that was decorated in 1829. Services are held here several times a day in Lithuanian, Polish and Latin. ⓐ Aušros Vartų 12 ☎ 5212 3513 🕐 07.30–18.30 daily

◯ The cathedral's bell tower is a striking landmark

The Dawn Gate

KGB Museum (Museum of Genocide Victims)

The former KGB and Gestapo headquarters and prison — a site of countless atrocities — now houses a stoic but chilling museum. There's no attempt to glorify or dress up the past, and there doesn't need to be. Descriptions on the walls simply state what each room was used for. The water torture room and padded cell are particularly quietening, but the execution chamber takes things to another level.

Entirely run by volunteers, the impressive no-nonsense set-up of the museum creates a completely appropriate and respectable representation of the grisly, painfully recent past. Outside the buildings, names of victims are engraved on the stones in the walls. At weekends, veterans can sometimes be seen gazing mournfully at the names and dates.

The KGB Museum is not the most pleasant sight you will see on your visit, but equally it is not to be missed. Note that while the museum is officially called the Museum of Genocide Victims

SEREIKIŠKIŲ PARK

A walk along the river through this central park is a real pleasure that can easily be fitted into a busy day. Find a spot on the bank under the shade of a tree and listen to the music of the river flowing by. If you're entering the park from Cathedral Square, pick up an ice cream from the stand as you walk in.

In the daytime, you'll often see couples and young families strolling through the grounds, or students sitting reading books. By early evening, however, a different crowd arrives and you'll notice that black leather, chains and large safety pins are still popular among some young people here.

(Genocido Aukų Muziejus), many believe this is an inappropriate name and it is generally referred to as the KGB Museum. ❸ Aukų 2a ❶ 5249 6264 ❿ www.genocid.lt/muziejus ● 10.00–18.00 Wed–Sat, 10.00–17.00 Sun, closed Mon & Tues ❶ Admission charge

St Anne's Church & the Bernardine Church

These two churches hug the same site. The attractive one closer to the street is St Anne's, an exquisite Gothic building that, allegedly, Napoleon wanted to hold in his hand and carry back to Paris. Thirty-three different kinds of decorative bricks were used in the construction,

⬤ The interior of the Bernardine Church

a unique method of building such a grand church and one which gives it a charming handmade appearance.

Next door is the Bernardine Church, fairly ordinary on the outside but hiding some real treasures inside. The best entrance is actually to the right of the main door by the bottom of the ramp. As your eyes grow accustomed to the dim light, look over to the left-hand wall and you'll see some frescoes which are unique in their combination of theme and style. The first and most impressive depicts St Christopher carrying a young Jesus across a river. Further into the church, along the same wall, you will notice some partially revealed confessionals.

The courtyard between the churches is lovely and a good place for romantic or family holiday snaps. If you see a 'no photography' sign on the gate, this is usually because a private formal event, such as a wedding, has just taken place. If you see the sign, just pop inside and ask at the souvenir stall if you may take photos.

❸ Maironio 8

CULTURE

Amber Museum-Gallery

Amber is the jewel of the Baltics – except when it contains a prehistoric insect, then it becomes compellingly curious and creepy. The Amber Museum-Gallery is really just a well-stocked shop with an excellent display downstairs showing off the main amber discoveries, different types of amber, and some inconceivably old preserved insects. Some could be 100 million years old, but their wings still look crisp in the hardened amber.

Also of note is an imitation display of the Juodkrantė Hoard, a famous collection of amber dredged up from the bottom of the

Curonian Lagoon by a mining company. Despite the fact that it contains evidence of the lifestyle of Stone Age Baltic tribes, the collection was quickly broken up and widely dispersed. This is one of the best amber museums in Lithuania, second only to the **Palanga Amber Museum** (Ⓦ www.pgm.lt) in the coastal town of Palanga. ⓐ Šv Mykolo 8 ❶ 5262 3092 ❶ 10.00–19.00 daily

Applied Arts Museum

One of the city's best museums for getting to grips with its illustrious and multi-ethnic past, this shouldn't be missed. What may at first look like a collection of rubble takes on new meaning when you discover something of its context, and then glance at the rapidly growing reconstruction site. There's also a fragment of the former city wall still visible in the basement.

The museum has an additional collection of art, mostly religious, dating from the 16th century. ⓐ Arsenalo 3a ❶ 5262 8080 ❶ 11.00–18.00 Tues–Sat, 11.00–16.00 Sun, closed Mon ❶ Admission charge

Higher Castle Museum (Gedimino Pilis)

The highlight – literally – of this museum is its tower, all that is left of the former castle and as iconic of Vilnius as anything in the city. A climb to the top will reward you with a terrific view over Vilnius's haphazard jumble of roofs. It's worth doing this towards the beginning of your stay in order to get your bearings. Bring your camera and binoculars if you have them.

The museum itself contains a collection of medieval decoration and artefacts. One of the most interesting displays is the model of how the whole castle complex originally looked. ⓐ Castle Hill, Arsenalo 5 ❶ 5261 7453 ❶ 10.00–17.00 Tues–Sun, closed Mon ❶ Admission charge

⬥ *The Amber Museum-Gallery features some excellent displays*

Kazys Varnelis Museum

The Lithuanian artist Kazys Varnelis spent a large amount of time in the US after escaping Soviet occupation in 1949. He focused on creating pattern-based optical illusion images on a large scale. He also collected a magnificent hoard of art and furniture covering a broad range of periods, cultures and styles.

When Varnelis returned to Lithuania in 1998, he brought his collection with him and arranged it carefully in this 33-room museum, in the order in which it remains to this day. ⓐ Didžioji 26 ⓣ 5279 1644 ⓛ 10.00–16.00 Tues–Sat, closed Sun & Mon ⓘ Advance reservation is required to visit the museum.

RETAIL THERAPY

Pilies Street is the place to find souvenirs, with shops ranging from ramshackle street-side affairs to clean, efficient stores with English-speaking staff. You will find plentiful amber and linen products as well as other tourist take-homes including T-shirts, flags and fridge magnets.

At the point where Pilies Street becomes Didžioji Street, there is a small market of stalls selling local artwork as well as more souvenirs. As with most markets in Lithuania, it's possible to haggle over the price here, although if sellers refuse to budge they really aren't going to let you change their mind.

TAKING A BREAK

Balti Drambliai £ ❶ Vegetarian café with a pleasant courtyard in summer. In winter, you'll have to burrow into the basement. ⓐ Vilniaus 41 ❶ 5262 0875 ⏲ 11.00–24.00 Mon–Thur, 11.00–04.00 Fri, 12.00–02.00 Sat, 12.00–24.00 Sun

Čili Kava £ ❷ Cheap and cheerful, with service at the counter. ⓐ Pilies 16 ❶ 5260 9028 ⏲ 07.30–22.00 Mon–Fri, 09.00–22.00 Sat & Sun

Coffee Inn £ ❸ Part of a chain of sandwich shops, serving good coffee but rather pricey sandwiches and wraps. Ideal for a quick break, especially if you prefer to see what your food looks like before making a selection. ⓐ Vilniaus 17 ❶ 6557 7764 ⏲ 07.00–22.00 Mon–Wed, 07.00–23.00 Thur, 07.00–24.00 Fri, 09.00–24.00 Sat, 09.00–22.00 Sun

Pilies Kepyklėlė £ ❹ A charming café littered with doilies and cream cakes in an excellent location. The salads, crêpes and pasta dishes are delicious. Try their speciality *medaus tortas* (layered honey cake) or the biscuity, fudge-filled *tinginys* ('lazybones' cake). Free Wi-Fi. ✆ Pilies 19 ☎ 5260 8992 🕐 09.00–23.00 daily

● *The view of the Old Town and Pilies Street*

Pizza Jazz £ ❺ One of the best outlets of this chain of classy pizza joints, where you can sip white wine or a cool beer while watching people stroll past the window. ❷ Vokiečių 24 ❶ 5212 3646 Ⓦ www.pizzajazz.lt ⓛ 11.00–23.00 Mon–Wed, 11.00–24.00 Thur, 10.00–02.00 Fri, 12.00–02.00 Sat, 12.00–23.00 Sun

Double Coffee £–££ ❻ Baltic-wide chain serving extremely good tea and coffee and a good range of salads, light meals, sweets and snacks. Rather pricey, but worth it for the choice. ❷ Vokiečių 3 ❶ 6502 7353 Ⓦ www.doublecoffee.lt ⓛ 08.00–22.00 Mon–Thur, 08.00–24.00 Fri, 09.00–24.00 Sat, 09.00–22.00 Sun

Blusyne ££ ❼ Tiny, quirky café, bar and restaurant in one, named after the owner's friendly dog. Ideal for coffee at any time but best in the evening for a meal or a glass of wine. There's outdoor seating in a secret little courtyard at the back in summer. ❷ Savičiaus 5 ❶ 5212 2012 Ⓦ www.blusyne.lt ⓛ 12.00–24.00 daily

Bobo ££ ❽ A microscopic café-bar serving good coffee, light snacks and an excellent range of imported beer. DJs often turn up in the evenings, which can get very long indeed. ❷ Trakų 15 ❶ 6777 7335 ⓛ 17.00–03.00 Mon–Thur, 13.00–05.00 Fri & Sat, 13.00–03.00 Sun

AFTER DARK

RESTAURANTS

Čagino ££ ❾ Drop in here for a Russian evening of food, vodka, music and loud laughter. It's a stylish brick-vaulted cellar with a tiled floor and can become very noisy when full. Food is both flavoursome and filling. You might be tempted to splash out on Russian vodka while you're here, but it's not necessary as Lithuanian vodka is much cheaper and generally just as good. The restaurant often closes for a month or two during the summer, moving to the seaside resort of Palanga. ⓐ J Basanavičiaus 11 ⓣ 5261 5555 ⓛ 12.00–24.00 daily

Dominikonų Karčema ££ ⓾ Honking great lumps of roasted meat sit alongside a range of healthier options in a classy albeit good value Lithuanian-Polish restaurant that also serves an excellent selection of local beers. ⓐ Dominikonų 6 ⓣ 6000 1977 ⓦ www.priekatedros.lt ⓛ 10.00–24.00 Mon–Wed, 10.00–01.00 Thur, 10.00–02.00 Fri, 12.00–02.00 Sat, 12.00–23.00 Sun

Graf Zeppelin ££ ⓫ A bargain-basement white-tablecloth affair knocking out the largest *cepelinai* (zeppelins) in the city. *Cepelinai*, the unofficial national dish, are as the name suggests blimp-shaped beasts of mixed mashed and grated potato with different fillings, which are boiled and served with a range of artery-clogging sauces. Other dishes of Lithuanian and German extraction are also available. ⓐ Savičiaus 9 ⓣ 6746 2949 ⓦ www.grafzeppelin.lt ⓛ 12.00–22.00 Mon–Thur, 12.00–23.00 Fri & Sat, 13.00–17.00 Sun

Saint Germain ££ ⓬ This long-standing restaurant's country-cottage charm makes it a favourite with loyal locals. The food is modest but creative in its garnishes and sauces. Ideal for romantic dinners, family meals or a special occasion. Advance booking is advisable. ⓐ Literatų 9, off Rusų ⓣ 5262 1210 ⓦ www.vynine.lt ⓛ 11.00–24.00 daily

Zoe's Bar & Grill ££ ⓭ This place burst on to the local dining scene and is now well into the swing of things. The food is American style with an occasional Asian twist, the atmosphere is bright and zesty, the service is bubbly and you're guaranteed a good feed and a fun night out. ⓐ Odminių 3 ⓣ 5212 3331 ⓛ 11.30–24.00 Mon–Wed, 11.30–01.00 Thur & Fri, 12.00–01.00 Sat, 12.00–23.00 Sun

Bistro 18 ££–£££ ⓮ Foreign run and with friendly staff, this is a favourite of trendy types who still like the comfort of home. Simple and stylish with a crisp but cosy atmosphere, the food is a mix of modern cuisine and home-style cooking. The little wine shop to one side has a great selection. ⓐ Stiklių 18 ⓣ 6777 2091 ⓛ 11.30–24.00 Mon–Fri, 17.00–23.00 Sat, 17.00–22.30 Sun

Helios ££–£££ ⓯ The Helios centre, right next to the Town Hall, contains a nightclub, steak restaurant, Japanese restaurant, casino and sports bar. All of them are excellent, if not at all Lithuanian. The nightclub is extremely modern and popular, while the restaurants offer some of the best international food in town. ⓐ Didžioji 28 ⓛ Opening times vary according to venue

Balzac £££ ⓰ The closest Vilnius comes to a real French bistro, Balzac hits the mark every time with the perfect blend of mix-and-match furniture and a changing menu of dishes made from fresh ingredients. ⓐ Savičiaus 7 ⓣ 6148 9223 ⓦ www.balzac.lt ⓛ 11.30–23.00 Mon–Thur, 11.30–24.00 Fri, 12.00–24.00 Sat & Sun

Lokys £££ ⓱ Opened in 1972, Lokys (The Bear) is one of Vilnius's oldest, most respected restaurants, famous for offering hunters' delights such as beaver as well as traditional Lithuanian dishes. Tables are in the cellars, accessed via a very narrow twisting stairway, and spread among various nooks, halls and little rooms, one of which used to be a prison cell. Wherever you choose to eat, the food is first class. On weekend evenings, they often put on medieval-themed music and entertainment. Ideal for groups or parties. Not to be confused with the steak restaurant of the same name on the ground floor. ❷ Stiklių 8 ❶ 5262 9046 ⓦ www.lokys.lt 🕙 12.00–24.00 daily

Medininkai £££ ⓲ Gorgeous rooms with arched ceilings decorated with intricate frescoes give this restaurant a fairy-tale feeling. The food is generally very good although certainly not cheap. Service is friendly if not always efficient. The best part of the experience is the special atmosphere, which offers an evening that won't be quickly forgotten. ❷ Aušros Vartų 8 ❶ 6008 6491 🕙 12.00–23.00 daily

Sue's Indian Raja £££ ⓳ This authentic Indian restaurant has justifiably attracted interest from international food and travel magazines. Meals are simple but beautifully prepared and consistently good. Icons in the menu indicate the degree of spiciness. Service is always friendly and efficient, and Raj, the owner, will often visit diners for a chat. ❷ Odminių 3 ❶ 5266 1888 ⓦ www.sues-lt.com 🕙 11.00–24.00 daily

Žemaičiai £££ ⓴ For an authentic adventure and some traditional food, this restaurant is hard to beat. The food is generally good and the rabbit-warren interior gives it a great atmosphere. When you enter, walk past the bar and head downstairs, taking care not to bang your head on the low ceiling. ❷ Vokiečių 24 ❶ 5261 6573 ⓦ www.zemaiciai.lt 🕙 11.00–24.00 daily

BARS & CLUBS
Amatininkų Užeiga Although it's technically a restaurant, regulars use the place as a bar. Notorious as the top place in town to eat

after a night of serious clubbing, summertime brings with it a vast terrace for the ultimate people-watching experience. **ⓐ** Didžioji 19 **ⓣ** 6872 2366 **ⓒ** 10.00–05.00 Mon–Thur, 10.00–07.00 Fri, 11.00–07.00 Sat, 11.00–05.00 Sun

Briusly Pronounced 'Bruce Lee', and inspired by his films, which were a black-market hit in the Soviet days, this place is frequently fizzing

▲ Take a stroll through the town

with fresh-faced happy people having a good time. Surplus to the bar on the ground floor, a small room in the cellar features DJs at the weekend. ❷ Islandijos 4 ☎ 5261 2753 ⏰ 11.00–24.00 Mon–Wed, 11.00–02.00 Thur, 11.00–06.00 Fri, 12.00–06.00 Sat, 12.00–24.00 Sun

Brodvėjus One of a few places that offer a fun and friendly atmosphere every night of the week. There's a lively bar downstairs and a lounge-style room upstairs. The mix of cacophonous and crazy on the one hand and the laid-back and mellow on the other is ideal. Meals are available. ❷ Mėsinių 4 ☎ 6525 7790 ⓦ www.brodvejus.lt ⏰ 20.00–04.00 Wed, 20.00–05.00 Thur, 20.00–06.00 Fri & Sat, 20.00–03.00 Sun–Tues

Cozy The cruisy café that sets the standard, popular with the young and trendy partly on account of the free Wi-Fi on offer. Smooth, slack style and good snacks and light meals are what it's all about. On weekend evenings, a DJ spins tunes in a cave-style lounge bar, attracting an easy-going and laid-back crowd of student types. ❷ Dominikonų 10 ☎ 5261 1137 ⓦ www.cozy.lt ⏰ 09.00–02.00 Mon–Thur, 09.00–04.00 Fri, 10.00–04.00 Sat, 10.00–02.00 Sun

Franki Franki has been one of the major successes of the last couple of years not least because it's one of the few places left in the capital where late-night drinking in a quiet atmosphere is still available. The service is a little random, but a visit is still recommended. Their summer terrace is just across the street at ❷ Šv Ignoto 5 and is a fine place to drink outside during the warmer part of the year. ❸ Vilniaus 37

🕿 5265 9999 🕐 10.00–03.00 Mon–Wed, 10.00–05.00 Thur–Sat, 11.00–03.00 Sun

In Vino Quintessential wine bar with a lovely local twist. Whether it be hot wine in winter, or a cool white on summer evenings in the courtyard, there's a relaxed, friendly and refined atmosphere to the place. ⓐ Aušros Vartų 7 🕿 5212 1210 Ⓦ www.invino.lt 🕐 16.00–04.00 Fri & Sat, 16.00–02.00 Sun–Thur

Mojito Naktys This cocktail bar is staffed by the sort of shakers who know the difference between a Classic Martini, a Vodka Martini and a Bradford. Frequented by a gently elite set of locals and expats, it's a groovy Vegas-style cave with an intricate cluster of little rooms scattered with padded benches and cushions. ⓐ Didžioji 33/2 (enter from Arklių Street) 🕿 6100 4131 Ⓦ www.mojitonaktys.lt 🕐 20.00–04.00 Thur, 21.00–05.00 Fri & Sat, closed Sun–Wed

Pabo Latino Top Latino club with exquisite decoration, a classy clientele, and, in summer, a courtyard for outdoor dancing and lounging about under tents. Dress smartly and expect queues at the door, although Thursday nights are a bit more casual and cheaper. ⓐ Trakų 3/2 🕿 5262 1045 Ⓦ www.pabolatino.lt 🕐 20.00–03.00 Thur, 20.00–05.00 Fri & Sat, closed Sun–Wed

Pramogų Bankas The casino's name means 'Entertainment Bank' and if you don't mind depositing a bit of cash you can make a whopping great withdrawal of fun. Aside from the casino, there are also a couple of bars and a swish restaurant inside. The top and bottom floors house nightclubs – head upstairs for dark lights and lasers or downstairs for a brighter vibe and a slightly older crowd. ⓐ Pamėnkalnio 7/8 🕿 7005

5555 Ⓦ www.pramogubankas.lt ⏱ 24 hrs; upstairs nightclub 22.00–06.00 Thur–Sat, closed Sun–Wed

Prospekto Klubas Dry by day, this place goes crazy at night and becomes one of the city's hottest clubs. Watch out for cheeky bartenders who 'assume' you want to leave tremendous tips and have your drinks mixed with top-shelf vodka. ⓐ Gedimino 2 ☎ 5212 0832 ⏱ 11.00–05.00 daily

Satta The brainchild of a Portuguese expat and the originators of Vilnius's original warehouse party scene, Satta is the only regular underground club in the city. Featuring cutting-edge DJs from home and abroad, this graffiti-splattered masterpiece is frowned upon by the conservative authorities and yet keeps on going. Find the entrance hidden away in a dark courtyard off the main street. ⓐ Vilniaus 16 Ⓦ www.satta.lt ⏱ Opening times depend on events; check website for details

Savas Kampas Simple, relaxed bar for catching up with friends and enjoying a drink and a snack. The two rooms at the back are dark but pleasant, with plenty of comfortable couches. Service can be slow, even by Lithuanian standards. ⓐ Vokiečių 4 ☎ 5212 3203 Ⓦ www.savaskampas.lt ⏱ 11.00–24.00 Mon–Wed, 11.00–01.00 Thur, 11.00–03.00 Fri, 11.00–02.00 Sat, 10.00–24.00 Sun

Woo A hotspot for youngsters looking for an underground garage feel, Woo is always swarming with groovy types on Friday and Saturday nights. There is an interesting menu of Asian snacks and meals. ⓐ Vilniaus 22 ☎ 5212 7740 ⏱ 11.00–02.00 Mon–Wed, 11.00–04.00 Thur, 11.00–06.00 Fri, 12.00–06.00 Sat, closed Sun

Užupis & Belmontas

The Užupis district is often described as having an alternative and arty aspect to it – something like Montmartre in Paris, Soho in London or Greenwich Village in New York. The reputation comes mostly from the fact that the area has half-mockingly declared itself an independent republic with its own constitution (see page 85).

The best time to visit Užupis is April Fools' Day, when the 'republic' celebrates its independence, will stamp your passport on entry, and provide all manner of entertainment for the day. At other times, the area is a charming collection of crumbling old buildings livened up by a celebrity statue of an angel. The term 'delightfully decrepit' has often been used to describe Užupis, as everything seems age-worn and weather-beaten – perfect for character-filled photographs. The Užupio Kavinė (see page 90) is the perfect place in Vilnius to have a beer by the river.

An afternoon spent in the area won't offer you much in the way of art and culture, particularly compared with the rich pickings in the Old Town, but it's a pleasant place for a quiet stroll. Visit with an open mind, and open eyes.

SIGHTS & ATTRACTIONS

Bernardinų Cemetery

Established in 1820 on a gradually eroding hill, some who were placed here for eternal rest have found the ground falling away beneath them. The cemetery contains the graves of university professors, scientists, artists and other intellectuals. You will notice that there are many Polish names on the tombstones. It's a beautiful place to visit in autumn and winter, when the ramshackle

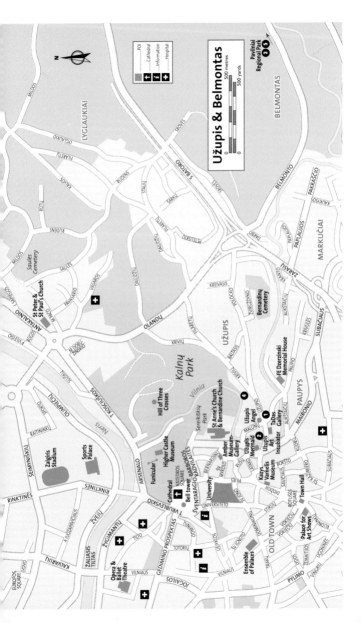

grounds and graves clinging to the eroding hillside are sprinkled with either golden leaves or snow. ❸ Žvirgždyno 3

Hill of Three Crosses

Right near Užupis, on the same side of the river and reached via Kalnų Park, is the iconic Hill of Three Crosses. Visible from most places in the Old Town, these three white crosses on top of a hill are laden with contradictory stories about their origin.

One story suggests that seven Franciscan monks were killed here by pagans, who tied them to the crosses then threw them down the hill into the river. The crosses may in fact have been erected to commemorate Vilnius being granted the Magdeburg Rights, which finally gave the town city status.

⬥ *The Three Crosses*

CONSTITUTION

As the Užupis area is something of a self-declared breakaway republic, residents have produced and ratified their own constitution. You can find the full text on a large plaque, proudly displayed on one of the walls that isn't crumbling, just a short wander down Paupio Gatvė in the opposite direction to the Užupis Angel. The constitution declares, among other things, that:

People have the right to die, but it's not a duty.
People have the right to be insignificant and unknown.
A dog has the right to be a dog.
People have the right to be misunderstood.

Stalin tore the original crosses down and had them buried, but you can see some of their wreckage as you climb up to see the shiny new ones. From the top of the hill, there is an excellent view over the city.

St Peter & St Paul's Church

This church is worth the trolleybus journey or 20-minute walk out of town. The interior is home to a couple of thousand gently cavorting characters – plaster stucco clinging to the walls and dripping from the ceilings. It's easily one of Vilnius's hidden treasures.

The building was commissioned in 1668 and a team of Italians worked their Baroque magic until the money ran out. Hence, the area around the altar is a bit plain in comparison to the rest of the interior. You'll also notice a chandelier ship floating overhead while you're in here, made from brass and a very impressive collection of clear glass marbles. It is a relatively recent addition to the church, made in Latvia in 1905.

ⓐ Antakalnio 1 ☎ 5234 0229 Ⓝ Trolleybus: 2, 3, 4, 14, 17 heading east

Užupis Angel & Užupis Mermaid

The most prominent feature of Užupis is an angel on a stick. It's certainly one of Vilnius's most amusing and pleasing sculptures, a breath of fresh air compared to some other rather austere statues. The statue of the angel that you can now see, balancing on a golden ball and silently blowing a trumpet across the rooftops, was unveiled on 1 April 2002.

Before the angel appeared, the plinth on top of the stick was adorned with a large egg. The egg was sold at auction and now rests on another stick, near the corner of Pylimo and Raugyklos streets. It was recently decorated with floral painting, making it look rather like a large Easter egg.

GRAFFITI TRAIL

Can you find the cartoon snail? Or what about the sign that says 'sky [dangus] – 12 km' under an arrow that points straight up? Stencilled, hand sprayed, or simply scrawled, the smattering of graffiti on the crumbling walls of Užupis adds a certain character to the area. Whether or not you are a fan of graffiti, you'll get a deeper insight into the local mentality if you take a closer look at some of the images and phrases displayed as you wander around.

◆ A vision of an angel

◓ *The floral egg on its nest*

The other notable statue in Užupis is the Užupis Mermaid (Užupio Undinė), set into a little cove in the wall of the river opposite the Užupio Kavinė café. One memorable winter morning she disappeared and was found some time later, carried downriver with the ice floes. It turned out that the ice forming around her bottom had squeezed her out of place and thrown her into the frozen river. She also took a dip when the river swelled during flooding in 2005.

WALKS

This area is great for peaceful strolling through streets and parks. Good walks are from the Užupis area to the Kalnų Park and the Hill of Three Crosses (see page 84), into Sereikiškių Park (see page 67), and also to St Peter & St Paul's Church (see pages 85–6). If you fancy a longer stroll, head out to Belmontas (see page 91). Invest in a detailed map to avoid getting lost, particularly in some of the parks.

For a walk combined with a bit of culture, start from the bridge where Užupio crosses the river, walk either over or under the outdoor seating deck of Užupio Kavinė, and then follow the river. Along here are some interesting artists' workshops. Some of the artwork, mainly sculpture, can be seen placed outside along the river. The workshops here are rather bohemian and opening hours vary wildly.

CULTURE

Užupio Meno Inkubatorius

The 'Užupio Art Incubator' as it translates represents Užupis in a nutshell. Anarchic, tumbledown and covered in graffiti, beyond the eccentricities found in and around the building are a few serious messages. Part arts centre and part gallery, all members of the local community as well as any passing foreigners are welcome to drop by and join in with the activities. Exhibitions are frequent plus there's an attached gift shop and the recommended club, Stopkė. ⓐ Užupio 2 ⓣ 6112 2675 ⓦ www.umi.lt ⓛ 11.00–18.00 Tues–Sat, 11.00–15.00 Sun, closed Mon

RETAIL THERAPY

Most of the shops in Užupis are the type that sell little other than cheese, lentils, beads and second-hand clothes. The alternative, anti-capitalist, anti-commercialism of Užupis means that gift and souvenir shops are thin on the ground, although one or two more upmarket interior decoration outlets are starting to pop up. Nothing is permanent in this area, so just take a stroll and see what you find.

TAKING A BREAK

Prie Angelo £ ❶ The cool little café right beside the angel is clean and fresh but still has an alternative feel to it. The furniture is wrought-iron artwork covered with cushions and there are a few angels stuccoed to the walls here and there. Pizzas and other more pleasing options are on the menu. ⓐ Užupio 9 ❶ 5215 3790 ❶ 09.00–24.00 Fri & Sat, 09.00–23.00 Sun–Thur

Užupio Kavinė £ ❷ A lovely spot to sit by the river and listen to the music of the water. Popular with locals in summer. The drinks are better than the food. ⓐ Užupio 2 ❶ 5212 2138 ❶ 10.00–23.00 daily

AFTER DARK

Joana Carinova Inn ££ ❸ Traditional Lithuanian meals are on offer in this impressive Belmontas restaurant bristling with stuffed animals and antlers. At weekends you can eat in a rather more civilised hall upstairs, but either way the food is excellent. ⓐ Belmonto 17 ❶ 6861 4656 ⓦ www.belmontas.lt ❶ 12.00–24.00 daily

BELMONTAS

Once a watermill with a small and shady inn on the side, this area has now become a huge complex of restaurants and relaxing spots. There are three restaurants here, including Joana Carinova Inn (see opposite) and Vila Gloria (see below), and plans for more.

Even if you don't fancy a meal, walking around the pleasant surroundings is a joy. You can explore the watermill itself as well as taking a walk through the Pavilniai Regional Park.

Belmontas is a good 40-minute walk from Užupis, most of it along the side of a narrow road. A taxi from the Old Town should cost no more than 25Lt.

Tores ££ ❹ There is only one venue of interest in Užupis after the sun goes down – Tores. Nestled on a hill overlooking the Old Town, the superb view alone is worth the visit. Service can be on the brusque side but don't let that spoil your evening. ❸ Užupio 40 ❶ 6553 2626 ❿ www.tores.lt ❹ 12.00–24.00 daily

Vila Gloria £££ ❺ This is the most upmarket restaurant in the Belmontas complex and the ideal venue if you want to splash out – not least because it has a small swimming pool in the middle of the dining room. The wine list is outstanding, but so are some of the prices. ❸ Belmonto 17 ❶ 6152 0220 ❿ www.belmontas.lt ❹ 12.00–24.00 daily

Central & New Vilnius

Outside of the Old Town, Vilnius loses much of its quaint charm but none of its interest. It's an area of contrasts. You'll see everything from gleaming glass office towers to some raw, brash outcrops of the Soviet era. You can dine in luxury, or see people pushing broken shopping trolleys at the market.

This area, coarse and real, is where things can take on a decidedly gritty and bizarre edge that's nonetheless worth a visit.

SIGHTS & ATTRACTIONS

Frank Zappa Statue

One of the more curious sculptures in Vilnius is that of the head of Frank Zappa, the deceased American musician and film director, mounted on a post. Zappa has nothing to do with Vilnius as such, but it was commissioned in 1995, two years after his death, by students in the city, who convinced authorities to allow it by arguing that Mr Zappa looked a bit Jewish. The sculpture was created by Konstantinas Bogdanas, who had previously honed his sculpting skills on the head of Lenin in Moscow. ❷ K Kalinausko 1

Parliament

The parliament buildings themselves are rather boxy and uninteresting, but head round to the west side of the complex to see a monument consisting of assembled blocks of concrete. These blocks were part of a barrier that was used to defend the parliament against Soviet tanks, which were trying to storm it in January 1991. ❸ Gedimino 53

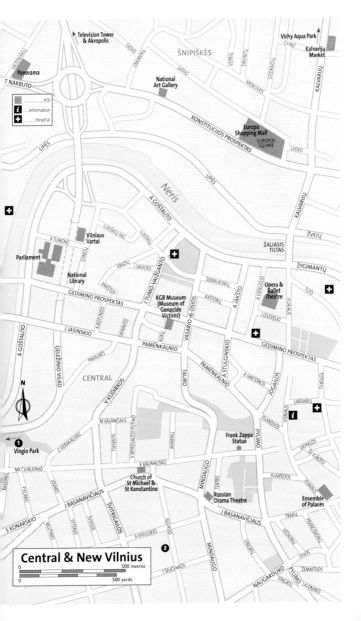

Central & New Vilnius

● *A tribute to the esteemed Mr Zappa*

St Michael & St Konstantine Church

This Orthodox church is most notable for the enormous green onions that stand out garishly against a blue sky, when there is one. What's behind the colour scheme, with its violent green roof, is a local mystery. ❷ Basanavičiaus 27

Vichy Aqua Park

Polynesian-themed aqua park filled with tangled water slides, a splashy kids' play area, a few pool bars, a wave pool, an artificial indoor beach and several saunas. You'll often see Polynesian performances taking place. It's all a bit plastic-fantastic, but certainly good fun. Surprisingly, it's especially nice in winter, when you can soak in a warm pool inside while snow piles up outside. ❷ Ozo 14c
❶ 5211 1653 Ⓦ www.vandensparkas.lt ⏱ 12.00–22.00 Mon–Thur, 10.00–22.00 Fri–Sun ❶ Admission charge

Žaliasis Tiltas (Green Bridge)

The first bridge to span the Neris was built here in 1536 and boasted a roof and shops. It has been damaged or destroyed and rebuilt several times, most recently in 1952. The current Green Bridge holds four statues that are the only remains of communist propaganda in Vilnius, constructed in the stern, proud style of socialist realism. *Agriculture* was sculpted by Bučas and Vaivada, *Industry* by Petrulis and Vyšniauskas, *Peace* by Pundzius and *Youth* by Mikėnas and Kėdainis. It's easy to look at them with a wry smile today and, given that they haven't been destroyed, decapitated or even defaced, one can only assume that the locals who lived under communism have learnt to do just that.

CULTURE

National Art Gallery

Opened in 2009, the city's new National Art Gallery puts on a range of local and international exhibitions focusing on everything from the late 19th-century painting from the Lithuanian Awakening to contemporary shows from international artists. ❷ Konstitucijos 22 ❶ 5219 5960 Ⓦ www.ndg.lt ❹ 12.00–19.00 Wed, Fri & Sat, 13.00–20.00 Thur, 12.00–17.00 Sun, closed Mon & Tues ❶ Admission charge

Russian Drama Theatre

This old-style theatre offers not just Russian drama, but also a wide variety of theatrical performances. The seating can be awkward but it is generally quiet and has an atmosphere of easy-going culture. Students often come here, reading a book while waiting for a performance to begin, and in some ways it feels a bit more honest

TELEVISION TOWER

The Vilnius TV Tower is the tallest building in Lithuania. At 326 m (1,070 ft) with the aerial included, it is even a couple of metres taller than the Eiffel Tower. The revolving café at the 165-m (540-ft) mark offers views over the city.

The main reason for visiting is historical. On 13 January 1991, the TV Tower punctured history when it became the centre of an assault by Soviet tanks. Thirteen unarmed Lithuanians were killed on that evening and many more were injured. The event provoked international outrage and condemnation and became a turning point in the collapse of the Soviet regime. There is a memorial and photographic exhibition at the base of the tower that is well worth a visit and a few moments of stoic silence. ⓐ Sausio 13-osios 10 ⓣ 5252 5333 ⓦ www.lrtc.lt ⓛ 10.00–21.00 daily ⓘ Admission charge (café only)

and genuine than a slick, modern theatre experience. Definitely worth a visit. ⓐ J Basanavičiaus 13 ⓣ 5262 0552 ⓦ www.teatras.lt

RETAIL THERAPY

Akropolis A large shopping centre with a wide range of fashion and food shops as well as one of the best bookshops in all of Lithuania. One shelf is dedicated to English-language books. Akropolis is also a good entertainment centre, with cinemas and an ice-skating rink thoughtfully placed in the middle. ⓐ Ozo 25 ⓣ 5248 1588 ⓦ www.akropolis.lt ⓛ Shops 10.00–22.00 daily; entertainment centre 10.00–24.00 daily

⬤ *Vilnius TV Tower with the Liberty Statue at night*

Europa This small, modern shopping centre, occupying the lower floors of a shiny elliptical tower, offers mostly fashion stores, a few restaurants and a supermarket. On the second floor, there are egg-shaped pods which provide interesting seating for some of the cafés. ⓐ Konstitucijos 7a ⓣ 5248 7070 ⓛ Shops 10.00–21.00 daily; restaurants 10.00–24.00 daily

Kalvarijų Market A stubbornly old-fashioned and authentic market experience in a city which is striving to become shiny and new. It's a huge outdoor expanse sprawling with stalls and swarming with bargain-hunters. Hours can be spent simply wandering around enjoying the hustle and bustle of it all, but keep in mind that some of the goods you purchase might not last that long. ⓐ Kalvarijų 61 ⓛ Early–13.00 Tues–Sun, closed Mon

🔾 Stock up on some local souvenirs

Panorama Just to the west of the city centre and arguably the best shopping and entertainment centre in Vilnius, Panorama boasts two floors of shopping plus an excellent Brazilian restaurant and an indoor go-cart track. ⓐ Saltoniškių 9 ① 5219 5811 ⓦ www.panorama.lt ① 08.00–23.00 daily

TAKING A BREAK

Vingio Park £ ❶ The enormous, untended park could occupy you for hours. In the middle is a huge arena which is often used for concerts. There's also a reasonable café-style restaurant behind the arena, with a small area for children to play in.

AFTER DARK

RESTAURANT

Fortas £ ❷ Fortas is cleverly divided into different areas for different styles of dining; you can come here to sit at the bar, slump on a sofa, or eat at a table that appears to be in someone's living room. The original concept was based on the British pub and is popular with locals and tourists alike. ⓐ Algirdo 17 ① 6520 1138 ⓦ www.fortas.eu ① 08.00–24.00 Mon–Fri, 11.00–24.00 Sat, 12.00–24.00 Sun

BARS & CLUBS

Bermudai Combining two treats in one, Bermudai, located in the cellar of the building that straddles the Baltasis Tiltas (White Bridge) over the Neris, serves a good range of beers produced in some of the country's best microbreweries as well as being a live music venue at the weekends. ⓐ Upės 6 ① 6557 0262 ① 12.00–24.00 Mon–Thur, 12.00–05.00 Fri, 15.00–05.00 Sat, 15.00–24.00 Sun

Gravity Gravity was a bomb shelter in days gone by and you'll still enjoy the novelty of entering through a long concrete tunnel. It used to be an iconic club in Vilnius but its heyday is passed – or else, the world's clubbing scene has moved on in terms of décor and lighting and left this one behind. The music is still good and international DJs are often billed, so it's worth a try even if the place feels a bit stale. ⓐ Jasinskio 16 ⓣ 6857 0350 ⓦ www.clubgravity.lt ⓛ 22.00–05.00 Thur & Fri, closed Sat–Wed

SkyBar The cocktail bar at the top of the Reval Hotel offers stunning views over the Old Town. Binoculars are available on request. The clientele are classy, so come dressed smartly to fit in. Prices are also sky-high, but it's worth it for an evening. This is also one of only a few places with a dedicated smoking room, popular since smoking in all restaurants, bars and clubs was banned at the start of 2007. ⓐ Konstitucijos 20 (Radisson Blu Lietuva) ⓣ 5231 4823 ⓦ www.revalhotels.com ⓛ 17.00–02.30 Fri & Sat, 17.00–01.00 Sun–Thur

Soho Now the only authorised gay club still operating in the city, Soho is very much a male-only affair. The two main areas are for drinking and other more intimate activities. The club has a good website with lots of information in English for those who'd like to find out more about upcoming events. ⓐ Švitrigailos 7/16 ⓣ 6993 9567 ⓦ www.sohoclub.lt ⓛ 22.00–04.00 Thur, 22.00–07.00 Fri & Sat, closed Sun–Wed

◗ *Trakai Castle*

OUT OF TOWN
trips

Trakai

If you've bought any postcards or coffee-table books full of pretty pictures of Lithuania, Trakai will need no introduction. It's the image of the gorgeous castle on an island in the middle of a lovely lake, which looks like something out of a fairy tale – and the real thing will not disappoint.

While there is no doubt that the castle is Trakai's central attraction, there's more to the town than that and it is certainly worth a half- or full-day trip.

Almost all visitors leave as the sun goes down as there are not many options for nightlife or accommodation – one of the best for both is the Apvalaus Stalo Klubas (see pages 109–10). Avoid going to Trakai on Monday and Tuesday when the main attractions are closed.

GETTING THERE

Trakai is about 25 km (15½ miles) from Vilnius, and can easily be visited in half a day. The most convenient option is to take a shuttle bus, organised either by your hotel or through a tour company.

A cheaper option is to go by regular bus. Buses to Trakai depart from Vilnius bus station roughly every hour with a journey time of around half an hour. The bus station is not near the town, so follow the road in the same direction as the bus was heading for about 20 minutes until you come across the main part of the settlement and the iconic castle.

A taxi from Vilnius to Trakai should cost around 90Lt, but it may be difficult to get a taxi back.

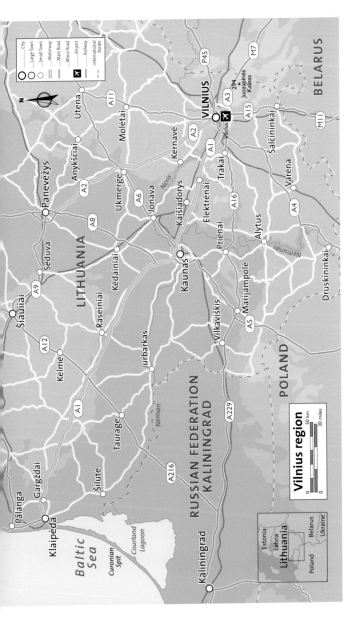

SIGHTS & ATTRACTIONS

Trakai Castle

Trakai Castle dates back to the 14th century but was almost completely destroyed during conflicts with the Russians in the couse of the 17th and 18th centuries. Restoration has been a stop-start affair since 1905.

Efforts made by imperial Russian authorities were interrupted by war, and the Soviet authorities subsequently decided that rebuilding the castle would be an inappropriate celebration of Lithuania's feudal past and brought the works to a halt again. Recent restoration took place in the 1980s and 1990s, giving the castle's magical, medieval appearance a fresh boost. The castle is used occasionally as a location for period dramas.

There is a worthwhile museum inside the castle, but just walking around the outside is also a pleasure. You can get a watery perspective by hiring a sailing boat (and someone to sail it) from the bridge leading up to the castle. ⓐ Pilies Island ⓣ 5285 3946 ⓛ 10.00–19.00 daily ⓘ Admission charge

CULTURE

Karaite Ethnographic Museum

Some will say they were 'invited' while others will say they were 'enslaved', but whichever way you look at it, a group of Karaite people from the Crimea came to Trakai in the 15th century to act as bodyguards for Lithuania's Grand Duke Vytautas. If you fancy more than a cursory glance at this fascinating community, a visit to the Karaite Ethnographic Museum is a must. ⓐ Karaimų 22 ⓣ 5285 5286 ⓛ 10.00–18.00 Wed–Sun, closed Mon & Tues ⓘ Admission charge

◆ *Preparing to sail past Trakai Castle*

THE KARAITE PEOPLE

A small community of the original Karaite immigrants' descendants still live in Trakai today and have managed to maintain their customs, culture and language. You can eat their food, look at their little coloured wooden houses (each of which has only three windows – one for God, one for the family and one for the Grand Duke), and sometimes see them standing by their front gates in traditional dress selling trinkets.

RETAIL THERAPY

As summer arrives along with the tourists, stalls pop up around the shores of the lake selling cheap sunglasses, jewellery, hot dogs, amber, ice creams and all manner of souvenirs. Note, however, that of all those items, the hot dogs will probably prove to be the best value and most durable. It's actually a credit to the community at Trakai that no more intrusive and permanent gift shops have blighted the pleasant little village.

TAKING A BREAK

The restaurants here (see pages 109–10) are dotted along the shore facing the castle, but one of the best options for eating and drinking in Trakai is to take a picnic. Why not eat your lunch and sip some bubbly on a gently drifting boat? Alternatively, stroll over to one of the less populated but equally pretty banks of the lake to enjoy the view in peace and quiet.

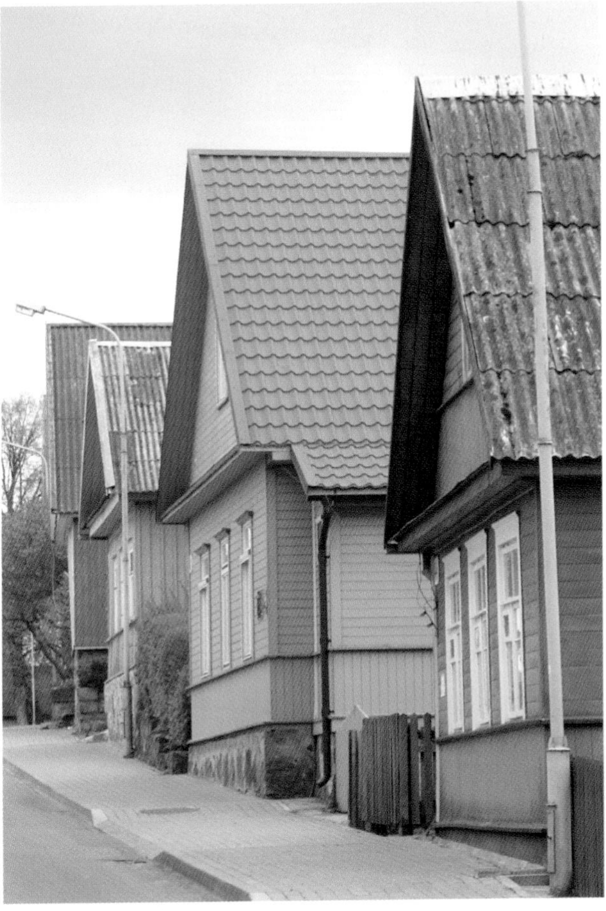

Traditional Karaite houses in a Trakai side street

⬥ *A beautiful sunset over the lake in Trakai*

Kybynlar £ This tastefully decorated little cottage offers a homely but not at all unsophisticated spot for lunch. It doesn't have a castle view but the cooking is above par for the area. *Kibinai* are served here also. ⓐ Karaimų 29 ⓣ 5285 5179 ⓛ 12.00–22.00 Mon, 11.00–22.00 Tues–Thur & Sun, 11.00–23.00 Fri & Sat

Senoji Kibininė £ While this place has a bit less to offer in terms of atmosphere, it is probably the best choice for trying *kibinai*, the traditional Karaite dish that can be found here. *Kibinai* are essentially hot, steaming pastry pockets full of spicy, juicy meat and onions. ⓐ Karaimų 65 ⓣ 5285 5865 ⓛ 10.00–22.00 daily

AFTER DARK

There is not much in the way of nightlife in Trakai, apart from the occasional rave-style event in summer. Watching the sun set over the castle is awesome, as is spending a few moments looking at the castle lit up after dark, but, unless you are satisfied with a quiet meal, there's no exciting reason to hang around.

Apvalaus Stalo Klubas ££ The name means the 'Round-Table Club', but they could also have justifiably called it the 'Best View'. The vista here is wonderful, looking out across the lake towards the castle. Bear in mind that the castle is lit in the evenings, so even an after-dark meal here is an experience.

There are actually two different restaurants in this same venue. Closer to the castle is the fine-dining restaurant, with fine linen, chairs wearing what look like dresses, and the best view of the castle to enjoy as you dine on French-style food. Nearby is a more casual pizzeria-style place offering pizzas and other dishes.

Weather permitting, there are plenty of places to sit outdoors and even a pontoon for meals afloat.

Accommodation is also available here in the form of romantic rooms overlooking the castle. ⓐ Karaimų 53a ⓣ 5285 5595 ⓦ www.asklubas.lt ⓛ Restaurant 12.00–22.00 daily; pizzeria 11.00–22.00 daily

Trakų Dvarkiemis ££ A massive modern building built along the lines of a traditional local manor house and dedicated to the art of hearty peasant food. The menu positively creaks with calories, plus there are facilities for children and a gift shop selling amber and other Lithuanian specialities. Find it on the main road just before you arrive in Trakai itself. ⓐ Užukampis village ⓣ 6188 8880 ⓦ www.trakudvarkiemis.lt ⓛ 11.00–01.00 Fri & Sat, 11.00–24.00 Sun–Thur

⬧ *Take a pleasant stroll around the castle*

Druskininkai

This is Lithuania's main spa-resort town, famed for its salty spring waters. The name Druskininkai comes from the Lithuanian word for salt (*druska*), and the whole town was formed around the salty springs. Local spas also specialise in mud, hot rocks, beating you with hot, wet branches, and other earthy forms of therapy and pampering.

In just the last few years, Druskininkai has been rapidly growing in popularity and earning quite a reputation not just for the health resorts, but also for active holidays and romantic weekends. New hotels have been popping up and the standard of service and accommodation has been steadily improving, although the homely, simple options still remain. Druskininkai successfully combines a basic and natural kind of appeal with as many, or as few, modern luxuries and conveniences as you may wish.

GETTING THERE

Druskininkai is roughly 130 km (80 miles) from Vilnius. There are several buses a day from Vilnius bus station to take you there. Keep in mind that some buses headed for Warsaw will pass through Druskininkai, adding to the options. Buses leave more frequently from Kaunas than from Vilnius, so if you're planning to visit Kaunas, it might be a good option to save your visit for there. As ever, check the timetables before you leave.

If driving, follow signs first to Kaunas, and then take the turn-off to Trakai. After that, there are signs to Druskininkai. Journey time is about two hours in a bus or an hour and a half by car.

◯ *Lake Druskonis is a peaceful spot*

SIGHTS & ATTRACTIONS

Architecture

Architectural contrast is a strong feature of Druskininkai and something to look out for. While parts of the town are being developed and appear shiny, new and fresh, there is still plenty of bizarre 1960s-style architecture to make wandering around town a fascinating visual experience.

Health resorts in the Soviet era were all, for some reason, made to look like concrete fossils of spaceships. For an excellent example, stroll around the building at Vilniaus 11, which has been developed into a sparkling water park but still retains many elements of the original architecture. Contrasting again with both the new buildings and the old Soviet constructions are the scattering of little wooden buildings, often covered in flaking coloured paint.

GRŪTO PARKAS (SOVIET STATUE PARK)

Nicknamed 'Stalinworld', this Soviet statue theme park is undoubtedly the single must-see attraction anywhere near Druskininkai or indeed anywhere near Vilnius. Many of Lenin's statues and a small selection of the Stalins that were scattered around Lithuania have ended up here. What is most interesting at Grūto Parkas, however, is not the towering communist statues themselves but the theme-park presentation of them, and the merrily mocking way the locals interact with the display.

In what can seem a curious turnaround, people who would once have shuffled grudgingly past these statues now turn up to pull faces at them, pose for photos, or just point and laugh.

⬤ *Communist statues in Grūto Parkas tell a story*

Such behaviour is, of course, not without controversy, but it seems that many Lithuanians have concocted a recipe for dealing with a miserable past that contains more humour than aimless hatred. It's something that those who never lived under the Soviet regime can't really claim to understand. But you can watch.

The statues are arranged unprotected along a path. You can go and stand beside them, put your handbag on their heads, pretend to be wiping their noses or ramming an umbrella into their ears. Most of the statues and busts are accompanied by a small panel with a photo and description of the original location. In the case of the huge statue of Lenin that stood in Vilnius's Lukiškių Aikštė, the now-empty 'Red Square' on Gedimino, there is a dramatic photo of the statue being knocked down. You can also see one of only three statues ever made of Lenin having a well-earnt sit down.

Also dotted along the path are guard towers that make a mockery of a concentration camp and speakers cranking out cheesy Soviet propaganda music. It all adds up to quite a strange experience. Be aware that much of the park is set around small lakes which attract swarms of blood-sucking mosquitoes in summer.

To get to Grūto Parkas, just mention the park to the driver of any bus that is going between Vilnius and Druskininkai and he will be happy to show you where to disembark. From the bus stop, it's about 1 km (⅔ mile) by foot down a signposted side road. ⓐ Druskininkai ❶ 3135 5511 ⓦ www.grutoparkas.lt ⓛ 09.00–17.00 daily ❶ Admission charge

⬥ *The park is full of imposing statues*

○ *A café in Druskininkai with a rustic setting*

CULTURE

Forest Echo Museum

This temple to wood — itself made of the material and set among trees by the side of the road — contains countless beautiful wooden creations from all over Lithuania. You'll see bus stops shaped like mushrooms, pagan 'totem' poles, wooden crosses, children's playthings shaped like animals and more. Don't forget to make a call on the wooden telephone while you're here. ⓐ Čiurlionio 116 ⓣ 3135 3901 ⓦ www.dmu.lt
ⓛ 10.00–18.00 Wed–Sun, closed Mon & Tues ⓘ Admission charge

TAKING A BREAK

If you're in Druskininkai, you're already taking a break. When you need to take a break from your break, try one of the following:

Regina £ A pleasant hotel restaurant, ideal for an evening meal with good company or a good book. ⓐ Kosciuškos 3 ⓣ 3135 9060
ⓦ www.regina.lt ⓛ 08.00–23.00 daily

Sicilia £ Essentially a pizza joint spread over two buildings — both places are casual and atmospheric and serve quality food. They are located near each other in a pleasant garden setting, one by a river.
ⓐ Taikos 9 & Čiurlionio 56 ⓛ 10.00–24.00 Fri & Sat, 10.00–23.00 Sun–Thur

AFTER DARK

Dangaus Skliautas £ Druskininkai has a way of sprinkling everything with strangeness and this place is certainly no exception. It's a low-key

restaurant most evenings, but can become interesting at the weekend when it transforms into a nightclub and you get tangled in the boudoir curtains that dangle about some of the dining booths. ⓐ Kurorto 8 ⓣ 3135 1819 ⓛ 11.00–24.00 daily

Salt Blues ££ Nightlife options remain thin on the ground in Druskininkai to say the least, meaning more often than not visitors need to use whatever facilities are available inside the town's hotels. Thankfully, this hotel bar, which also doubles as a fairly decent international restaurant, is better than the average hotel bar. As well as serving a remarkably good pint of draught Guinness®, there's also a large terrace which opens during the summer affording a splendid view of the nearby river. ⓐ Vilniaus 7 (Europa Royale hotel) ⓣ 3134 2221 ⓛ 11.00–24.00 daily

ACCOMMODATION

Regina ££ They've got the balance of uncomplicated comfort just right here – it's pleasant enough for a weekend away with someone special, while also affordable. The hotel also offers some very attractive package deals that include the use of the health resort and spa facilities. ⓐ Kosciuškos 3 ⓣ 3135 9060 ⓦ www.regina.lt

Spa Vilnius Sana ££ From the outside, this health spa looks like something that just fell to earth from space. It's the place to come for a 'trip' into health land, where they can not only put you up for the night, but also smother you in mud, massage you with rocks and so on. ⓐ Dineikos 1 ⓣ 3135 3811 ⓦ www.spavilnius.lt

Europa Royale £££ A renovated 18th-century manor is now home to one of the most swish hotels in town, with rooms that come complete with an abundance of luxury. ❸ Vilniaus 7 ❶ 3134 2221 Ⓦ www.groupeuropa.com

⬥ Druskininkai's Russian Orthodox church

Klaipėda

Lithuania's coastal region centres around the seaport of Klaipėda, the former Prussian city of Memel. It's a long way from Vilnius – 300 km (186 miles) as the crow flies and nearly four hours on a bus or five on the train – but worthwhile if you are spending any more than a short time in Lithuania. It's particularly attractive in summer.

From Klaipėda, you can easily visit either the Curonian Spit or Palanga. The Curonian Spit (see pages 124–5) is a long finger of land that pokes out from Kaliningrad into the Baltic Sea and comes close to touching Klaipėda at its tip. The top half of the spit is Lithuanian territory, while the bottom half is Russian. The entire Curonian Spit is an area of unique and beautiful nature, and tends to be very tranquil even in summer. Palanga is a crowded, raucous beach-and-party town in summer and a popular destination for those looking for easy fun. In off-peak seasons, it is a pleasant and quiet village in a lovely seaside location.

GETTING THERE

Scores of buses and minibuses leave daily for Klaipėda from Vilnius, taking on average four hours to make the trip. Don't make the mistake of getting on one of the few daily buses that snakes its way to the coast via numerous towns and villages and taking up to eight hours to complete the journey. The faster buses, which still make at least one short stop on the trip, are marked Ekspresas on timetables. The excellent website at ⓦ www.autobusubilietai.lt includes all buses and can even sell tickets online.

⬥ A constant military presence in Klaipėda

Three trains travel from Vilnius to Klaipėda every day, taking up to five hours to make the trip. Although longer, the train is preferable if you want to see something of the rest of the country. The bus simply goes through the middle of the countryside while the train stops at several towns along the route. For more information about train times in Lithuania, see ⓦ www.litrail.lt

SIGHTS & ATTRACTIONS

Amberton Klaipėda

The huge Amberton Klaipėda building was built in two halves forming a 'K' shape. Zip up to the 21st floor for spectacular views of the city and the tip of the Curonian Spit. There's a café and restaurant at the top but the food is rather overpriced – it's best to feed your hungry eyes on the surrounding landscape instead. ⓐ Naujojo Sodo 1 ⓣ 4640 4372 ⓦ www.ambertonhotels.com ⓛ 12.00–03.00 daily

Cat & Mouse

Tucked away in the heart of the Old Town are two little statues that are sure to raise a smile. The exact locations are kept secret as stumbling across them or trying to find them is half the fun. The cat sculpture (by the sculptor Midvikis) appears to have prosthetic limbs and a splendid moustache, and the mouse (by Plotnikovas and Jurkus) proudly displays radar-dish ears. The mouse will, allegedly, listen to your wishes if you whisper into its ears.

The Curonian Spit

Many of the best attractions and distractions around Klaipėda are not in the town itself but on the Curonian Spit. A passenger ferry (ⓐ Žvejų 8 ⓣ 4631 1117 ⓦ www.keltas.lt) shuffles to and from the

> **HILL OF CROSSES**
> One advantage of travelling to Klaipėda on the earlier train is
> that it will stop in Šiauliai at about 09.20. This is home to the
> famed Hill of Crosses and you can easily get off the train in
> Šiauliai, visit the hill, spend some time exploring Šiauliai itself,
> and then continue on to Klaipėda. Trains from Šiauliai to
> Klaipėda conveniently leave at 15.48 (arriving at 18.35) and
> 20.08 (arriving at 22.05).
>
> The **Šiauliai tourist information office** (☎ 4152 3110
> ⊛ http://tic.siauliai.lt) will also be able to help in planning a visit,
> including making arrangements for a taxi to the Hill of Crosses.

town and the spit on a pretty much non-stop basis, although you
should check the last return time. You should not count on getting
back much later than 23.00 in summer.

The return ferry ride from Klaipėda to the Curonian Spit costs
around 2Lt. Bikes are charged at 2Lt extra. When the ferry docks at
Smiltynė, there will be various buses and taxis offering to take you
down the spit to Juodkrantė and Nida (see below), the two main
destinations along the way.

To get across in a car, follow the signs to the more southern
car-only ferry terminal, about a five-minute drive out of town at
Nemuno 8. The basic fare for a car and driver is 40Lt with extra
charges for each passenger.

Nida dunes
If it were not covered in all those hand-planted pine trees, the
whole Curonian Spit (see opposite) would just blow away. As such,

there are not many parts of the spit that are not wooded, but you can still see the beautiful naked dunes just south of Nida. It's well worth exploring the area as it gives you not just stunning views but a good sense of just how fragile the whole area is.

Stick to the numerous paths – if you follow them in a general upwards direction you'll come across an old sundial. This broken obelisk, sticking out of an arrangement of various tiles, was smashed to pieces by a hurricane some time ago. You can still see, however, the engravings of ancient-looking runes around the dial.

Looking south from the sundial you are actually looking into Russia. If you've got good eyes, a good zoom lens or binoculars, you will be able to make out a line of black flags sticking out of the dunes marking the border.

Sea Museum

A short walk to the right from the passenger ferry will take you to the Sea Museum, which consists of some outdoor attractions (old boats, old shacks) and the big crowd pleaser – the aquarium. Housed in a rather curious building that was once a fort, you will find all manner of fishy things to feast your eyes on, including sharks, ravenous piranha, electric eels and invisible deadly jellyfish. The interior of the building itself is also fun and the kids will love the performing dolphins and sea lions. ⓐ Smiltynės 3 ❶ 4649 0754 ⓛ 10.30–18.30 daily ❶ Admission charge

Simon Dach Fountain

The German poet Simon Dach (1605–51) is commemorated by a fountain that contains a statue of Aennchen von Tharsus.

⬥ *Great views of the city from the Amberton Klaipėda Hotel*

⬭ Klaipėda's very own guard dog!

She was the subject of an East Prussian love song that was thought to have been composed by Dach. The sculpture was originally crafted by Berlin sculptor Alfred Kune and erected in 1912, but it disappeared during World War II and was never heard of again. The version you see now was re-created in 1989 based on old photos. ❷ Teatro Aikštė

CULTURE

Castle Museum
The port area in which the Castle Museum is located is changing by the day. The museum itself is hidden under a grassy mound but, fortunately, the entrance is well marked. Inside, you can see objects relating to the history of the region from the 16th century to the present day. Excavation works are taking place outside, revealing some of the original foundations of the fort. It's possible to wander around and get a sense of history being dug up before your very eyes. ❷ Pilies 4 ❶ 4641 0527 ❸ 10.00–18.00 Tues–Sun, closed Mon ❶ Admission charge

Witches' Hill
This is where three important Lithuanian traditions come together, namely, woodcarving, paganism and the tendency to act a little bit crazy. The result is the Witches' Hill, or 'Raganų Kalnas'. It consists of a path leading over the wooded dunes and dotted with various strange carved characters with enormous tongues, wild hair, big bulging eyes and all manner of other peculiar features. With the wind whispering through the pines, shadows flitting across the sandy path, and such goggle-eyed ghouls looking at you, it can verge on being a bit creepy.

FESTIVAL CITY

The biggest cultural event of the year is the Klaipėda Sea Festival, held in summer each year, generally towards the end of July. For three days the city streets flood with people enjoying concerts, all manner of outdoor eating and drinking venues, stalls, markets, performances and more. If you do want to visit during the Sea Festival, be sure to book accommodation well in advance. Check Ⓦ www.klaipedainfo.lt for exact dates and a programme of events.

Summer is the time when Klaipėda really comes alive, if in an unpredictable way. Temporary stages pop up in outdoor spaces, particularly in the big apron at the back of the Amberton Klaipėda and on the green triangle of land at the intersection of Tomo and Mėsininkų. You might also come across performances in the grassy area by the lagoon shore in Juodkrantė.

A jazz festival is held every year in early June. See Ⓦ www.jazz.lt

All the statues here were created by local artists and the collection started coming together in 1980. It has grown over the past three decades to become one of the main tourist attractions on the Curonian Spit.

RETAIL THERAPY

Klaipėda is not the finest town for shopping, but it has enough to keep kids amused and you stocked up with supplies. It's best to head for one of the shopping centres.

Akropolis Similar to the Akropolis in Vilnius (see page 96), this vast shopping centre also boasts cinemas and an ice-skating rink. It makes for a pleasant break from the summer heat. ⓐ Taikos 61 ⓦ www.akropolis.lt

Big The claim that Big is the biggest shopping centre around is a bit dubious, but it's fine for all the usual chains. ⓐ Taikos 139 ⓣ 4627 7499 ⓦ www.big-klaipeda.lt

Herkaus Galerija The latest city-centre shopping centre features a clutch of retail outlets aimed at the fashion market plus a couple of restaurants. ⓐ Manto 21

TAKING A BREAK

A J Šokoladas £ A small café notable for also selling a fabulous range of handmade chocolates from Trakai. ⓐ Karoso 9 ⓣ 6187 7199 ⓛ 09.00–19.00 Mon–Fri, 10.00–16.00 Sat, closed Sun

Bis £ A charming little café inside the Klaipėda Concert Hall selling drinks and light meals. The summer terrace is a really nice place to relax when the weather is good. ⓐ Šaulių 36 ⓣ 4625 6421 ⓛ 09.00–22.00 daily

Čili Kaimas £ Tucked under a hideous concrete box of a former cinema is Klaipėda's very own Čili Kaimas restaurant. The recipe here is exactly the same as that used to ensure success in Vilnius (see pages 146–9): efficient service, cheap but good-quality food, and oodles of calories. ⓐ Manto 11 ⓣ 4631 0953 ⓦ www.cili.lt ⓛ 11.00–02.00 Fri & Sat, 11.00–23.00 Sun–Thur

Kuršis £ This restaurant is open throughout the year so definitely not a tourist trap and very popular with the locals – a smart place opposite the bus station and specialising in classic Lithuanian dishes. It is also a great place to sit and relax outside with a drink and while the afternoon away. ⓐ Naglių 29, Nida ⓣ 4695 2804 ⓛ 09.00–24.00 daily

Senoji Hansa £ This small chain of otherwise unremarkable cafés has one location right near the main square in the Old Town, and is therefore well worth seeking out. In summer, a canopy covers an outdoor seating area which always proves popular – so much so that they can, at times, struggle to provide good service. Food is both cheap and edible, but just relaxing with a drink and a snack seems to be the norm here. ⓐ Kurpių 1 ⓣ 4640 0056 ⓛ 09.00–01.30 Mon–Fri, 10.00–01.30 Sat & Sun

Navalis £–££ Spilling out from beneath one of the city's smartest hotels is an equally smart café where you can enjoy coffee, croissants, snacks and a spot of people-watching. ⓐ Manto 23 ⓣ 4640 4200 ⓦ www.navalis.lt ⓛ Café 08.00–24.00 daily; restaurant 12.00–24.00 daily

Ešerinė ££ If you find yourself somewhere near Nida towards the end of the day, you could do a lot worse than take refuge beneath one of these island-style grass huts and order fish. The food is expensive here, but as is often the case you get what you pay for. Enjoying delicious seafood with such a nice view across the lagoon is a rare pleasure. ⓐ Naglių 2, Nida ⓣ 4695 2757 ⓛ 10.00–24.00 daily

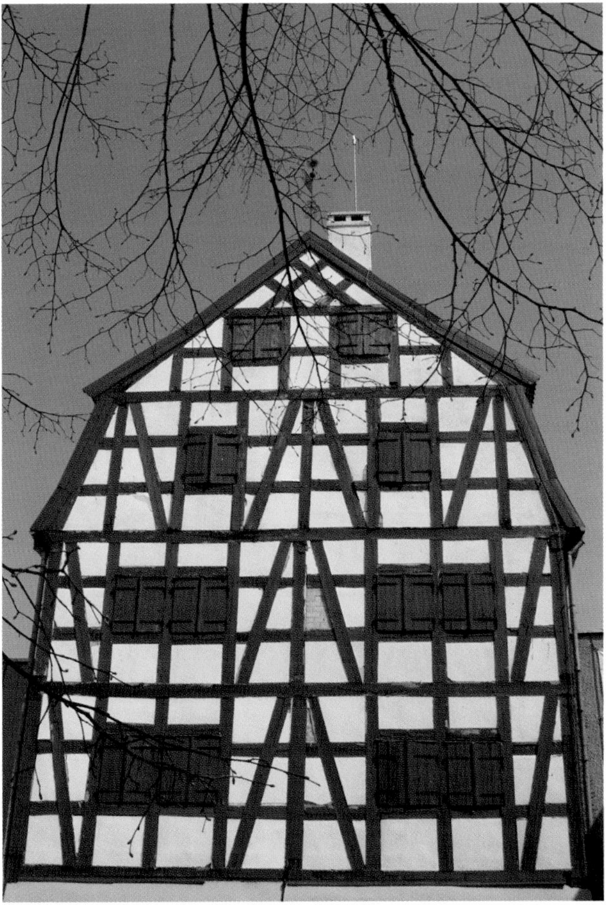

Distinctive wooden architecture in Klaipėda

AFTER DARK

RESTAURANTS

Memelis ££ An old warehouse facing the river has been turned into a fun-house for grown-ups and features a combined restaurant and beer hall on two floors. The menu focuses on fish and German cuisine, in keeping with the traditions of the region and the history of the building. The owners brew their own beer and are happy to

⬤ *The popular Memelis brewery and restaurant*

serve it in ridiculous portions, including tall four-litre glass tubes with little taps at the bottom. The aim is to set it up on the edge of the table and lie underneath it with your mouth open. ⓐ Žvėjų 4 ⓣ 4640 3040 ⓦ www.memelis.lt ⓛ 12.00–03.00 Fri & Sat, 12.00–24.00 Sun–Thur

Skandalas ££–£££ Crammed with corny, American Route-66 kitsch such as number plates, old advertisements and even a bronze Statue of Liberty, this American-style restaurant serves generous, simple and tasty meals. The place buzzes with a fun and friendly crowd at weekends. It's a bit of a stroll away from the centre, but well worth finding. ⓐ Kanto 44 ⓣ 4641 1585 ⓦ www.skandalas.info ⓛ 12.00–01.00 Mon–Thur, 12.00–02.00 Fri & Sat, 12.00–24.00 Sun

BARS & CLUBS

ElCalor One of Klaipėda's best Latino clubs, offering dance classes and demonstrations throughout the evening as well as music and dancing. The atmosphere is rather gaudy and the dance floor can get crowded, so watch you don't get pushed down the stairs into the toilets. ⓐ Kepėjų 10 (entrance on Jono) ⓣ 4631 3645 ⓦ www.elcalor.lt ⓛ Opens for events; call or check website for details

Eldorado Completely overhauled and now more of an exclusive restaurant with parties for 40-somethings during the weekends, Eldorado is Lithuanian bling at its best. The food looks good but tastes average, meaning drinking is the best option here. A large screen also makes it a popular place to visit during important basketball matches. ⓐ Lietuvninkų 2 ⓣ 4633 3333 ⓛ 10.00–24.00 Mon–Wed, 10.00–01.00 Thur, 10.00–02.00 Fri, 11.00–02.00 Sat, 11.00–24.00 Sun

Kalifornija A Klaipėda legend located in a Soviet housing estate in the far south of the city, Kalifornija isn't for the faint-hearted. Fuelled on copious amounts of vodka and, increasingly, techno, the girls wear little and the boys are less menacing than they look. ⓐ Laukininkų 17 ⓣ 4622 9735 ⓛ 23.00–07.00 daily

Paradox A hotspot for young, often underage, clubbers, this rather tacky place has a Russian-kooky feel to it. ⓐ Minijos 2 ⓣ 6877 7001 ⓛ 22.00–05.00 Fri & Sat (hours vary), closed Sun–Thur

Roxy Close to the bus station to the north of the city centre, Roxy panders to the city's student population with a mixture of themed nights and live music events. ⓐ Priestočio 9 ⓣ 6719 9998 ⓦ www.roxyclub.lt ⓛ 22.00–05.00 Thur–Sat, closed Sun–Wed

Šikšnosparnio Lizdas (Bat's Nest) A hotspot for Goths as well as the curious, this club has a cave-like atmosphere with lots of creative touches, including 'windows' set into each table displaying pieces

THE BEST JAZZ CLUB IN LITHUANIA

Kurpiai is often touted as the best jazz club in Lithuania and with good reason. Even when it hasn't attracted the hottest acts, it's a fun place to drop in and spend an evening. There is a wacky layout that makes the place feel that it was just chucked together, and the sort of atmosphere in which people who didn't arrive together nevertheless end up dancing with one another. ⓐ Kurpių 1a ⓣ 4641 0555 ⓦ www.jazz.lt ⓛ 12.00–24.00 Mon & Tues, 12.00–01.00 Wed & Thur, 12.00–04.00 Fri & Sat, 18.00–24.00 Sun

of old iron gadgets. A fun place to settle in for the evening, although you may want to avoid it on a full moon. ⓐ Tiltų 5 ❶ 4631 3412 🕐 11.00–24.00 Mon–Sat, 12.00–24.00 Sun

🔺 *An ornate façade in Klaipėda*

ACCOMMODATION

Klaipėda Keliautojė Namai Hostel £ Conveniently right next to the bus station. While things are very basic here (just a couple of rooms crammed with bunks), it is a friendly and easy-going place. Take a clothes peg, as there is a no-shoes policy, which has the expected effect in summer. ⓐ Butkų Juzės 7/4 ⓣ 4621 1879 ⓦ www.klaipedahostel.com

Aribė ££ Excellent three-star accommodation close to the city centre, the rooms are clean if nothing fancy, plus there's free wireless Internet throughout and a buffet breakfast. ⓐ Bangų 17a ⓣ 4649 0940 ⓦ www.aribe.lt

Litinterp ££ As is the case in Vilnius and Kaunas, Litinterp in Klaipėda offers simple, clean and comfortable accommodation at reasonable prices. The location is excellent given the price, but they can also organise home stays and accommodation in Nida and Palanga. ⓐ Puodžių 17 ⓣ 4641 0644 ⓦ www.litinterp.com

Amberton Klaipėda ££–£££ This landmark hotel shows what can be done with an old Soviet-style tower, plenty of money, and some fancy interior designers who know what to do with dark wooden panels, moody lighting and flat-screen televisions. If you can afford it, you won't regret it. ⓐ Naujojo Sodo 1 ⓣ 4640 4372 ⓦ www.ambertonhotels.com

● *Railway sign above Vilnius station tracks*

PRACTICAL
information

Directory

GETTING THERE

By air

At the time of writing, there were no direct flights between Vilnius and the UK. Low-cost airline **airBaltic** (Ⓦ www.airbaltic.com) is the best option, providing flights connecting in either Copenhagen or Rīga. The Eastern European budget carrier **Wizz Air** (Ⓦ www.wizz air.com) and several others have announced that they are filling this gap with the introduction of seven new routes in April 2011. Alternatively, **Ryanair** (Ⓦ www.ryanair.com) operates several flights a week between Kaunas and Bristol, Edinburgh, Liverpool and London Gatwick. A connecting bus service picks up passengers at Kaunas Airport and delivers them to the centre of Vilnius in about 90 minutes.

Many people are aware that air travel emits CO_2, which contributes to climate change. You may be interested in the possibility of lessening the environmental impact of your flight through **ClimateCare**, which offsets your CO_2 by funding environmental projects around the world. Visit Ⓦ www.jpmorganclimatecare.com

By rail

The preferred mode of transport in Lithuania is the bus, making travelling by train something of an adventure. Getting to Lithuania by train from Western Europe is not easy. The route needs a change of train in Warsaw, which connects with one daily train between the Polish and Lithuanian capitals – a spartan affair with no facilities that takes ten hours to make the journey. Connections with Belarus and Russia on the other hand are excellent. Full timetables in English can be found online at Ⓦ www.litrail.lt

By road

Regular buses ferry travellers between Vilnius and the other Baltic capitals and are ideal for those who are also visiting Latvia or Estonia. Buses are also a good way of travelling to and from cities in Poland and further west. **Eurolines Baltic International** (ℹ 5233 6666 ⓦ www.luxexpress.eu) has connections to most European cities including an overnight bus to London.

● *Navigate your way around Vilnius*

By sea

Ferries run by **DFDS Lisco** (☎ 4639 3600 ⓦ www.dfdslisco.lt) travel to Klaipėda from Kiel and Sassnitz in Germany and Karlshamn in Sweden. Klaipėda's international ferry terminal is a good 30 minutes south of the city.

ENTRY FORMALITIES

Lithuania has been a member of the EU since 2004 and a member of the Schengen Agreement since 1 January 2008, so former travelling restrictions have melted away. Citizens of the European Union, United States, Canada, Australia and New Zealand do not require a visa for stays of under three months within a year. Citizens of other countries do require a visa and health insurance. Exact details, including visa application procedures, are on the website of the **Lithuanian Ministry of Foreign Affairs** (ⓦ www.urm.lt).

EU citizens have few incoming customs restrictions except for temporary restrictions sometimes imposed for health and safety reasons. There is a limit of €10,000 in cash. Non-EU citizens are limited to bringing in 1 litre of spirits or 2 litres of wine or beer; 200 cigarettes or 100 cigarillos or 50 cigars or 250 g of tobacco. Non EU-citizens are also limited to 50 ml of perfume or 250 ml of eau de toilette.

MONEY

The Lithuanian currency is the litas (Lt), pegged to the euro at an exchange rate of 3.45Lt to €1. The rule of thumb for UK travellers is 4Lt to £1. Euros are not widely accepted, except for in a handful of shops in the centre. Sterling and US dollars are not accepted at all. Currency can be changed at bureaux de change at the airport and train stations as well as at many locations in the Old Town, including casinos.

The easiest way to withdraw money is through an ATM machine. ATMs are abundant in Vilnius, including at the airport, bus and train stations, but can be less common in smaller villages. Take plenty of cash if you are planning an out-of-town adventure.

Credit cards (MasterCard and Visa) are widely accepted in larger stores, but be aware that smaller or new businesses will often only accept cash.

HEALTH, SAFETY & CRIME

Tap water is perfectly safe to drink in Vilnius. The standard of public healthcare is improving but hospital facilities may not appear to be up to Western standards and tend to suffer from corruption. Bring a European Health Insurance Card (EHIC Ⓦ www.ehic.org.uk) for free or reduced-cost treatment in public clinics and hospitals. Private clinics abound, catering to a growing stream of health tourists from the UK who come here for operations, and the quality of service they provide is often world class. See page 154 for more details.

Police in Lithuania are fairly stern and not generally helpful to tourists who ask the time or for directions. They should, however, be your first point of contact if you are the victim of theft or violence. They are dressed in green and always work in pairs, one of whom is supposed to speak English. While this is rarely the case in reality, the situation is improving.

Vilnius Old Town is generally a very safe place to visit and pickpocketing is not as common here as it is in most European cities these days. As usual, however, you should exercise caution by sticking to well-lit streets in the Old Town at night and by keeping a sharp eye out for potential problems, including keeping your drink with you at all times. Leave valuables safely locked up at your hotel and avoid any late-night invitations to someone's home.

Lithuanians have a reputation for being racist, and although this is not true for all locals there are sometimes cases of dark-skinned visitors being turned away from nightclubs.

However you book your city break, it is important to take out adequate personal travel insurance for the trip. For peace of mind, the policy should give cover for medical expenses, loss, theft, repatriation, personal liability and cancellation expenses.

If you are travelling in your own vehicle, you should also check that you are appropriately insured. Make sure you take relevant insurance documents and your driving licence with you and leave photocopies of them in a safe place.

OPENING HOURS

Opening hours can vary wildly in Lithuania, particularly in more rural areas. Standard business hours are 09.00–18.00 and restaurants are generally open 12.00–24.00. Grocery stores and supermarkets are mostly open 07.00–22.00 daily.

Nightlife happens late – many nightclubs might not even open until 22.00 and don't get going until 24.00. At weekends, nightclubs close at about 05.00, and then many people simply head to one of the all-night cafés or bars. Vilnius is a city that doesn't encourage sleep.

Opening hours are usually printed on the doors of shops and restaurants, sometimes as a line of blocks or Roman numerals, one representing each day of the week from Monday (I) to Sunday (VII).

⬤ *A Vilnius government building*

TOILETS

The horrors of squatting have ceased. These days you'd have to go out of your way to find an old-fashioned Soviet-era toilet. Clean public toilets charging a small fee are scattered around a few parks and streets in the city. If there's not one nearby, the best option is to head into a café or hotel foyer and – if you have no intention of buying a coffee or becoming a customer – to ask politely.

Be careful of the gender signs. The gents is marked with a triangle which is broad at the top and pointed at the bottom (think 'broad shoulders') while the ladies is the other way round (think 'skirt'). You might also see 'V' for men (*vyrų*) and 'M' for women (*moterų*). The international 'WC' is used to signpost toilets.

CHILDREN

Children will be welcome in Vilnius as much as in any Western city. There are children's play areas in the parks, but you should be aware that the equipment in them is not as well maintained as you might like. There are no health-and-safety watchdogs here.

It's not common to find baby-change facilities or high chairs in shops, cafés or restaurants. Nappies and other baby supplies, however, are all available in supermarkets (see page 26).

An ideal day out for older kids is a trip to the Akropolis shopping and entertainment centre (see page 96). It's home to a handy ice-skating rink, as well as cinemas, plenty of restaurants, and of course shops. Films are generally shown in the original language with Lithuanian subtitles, but do check before buying a ticket.

For a restaurant with a child-friendly twist, try **Čili Kaimas** (ⓐ Vokiečių 8 ⓣ 5231 2536 ⓦ www.cili.lt ⓒ 11.00–02.00 Fri & Sat, 11.00–24.00 Sun–Thur). Downstairs, there's a large pool stocked with fish which will keep kids amused for hours, as will the live

◆ *Higher Castle can easily be reached by funicular railway*

◯ *Amber jewellery is popular with tourists*

chickens near the entrance upstairs and the grass snake near the toilets. There's also a *babushka* – a Russian-style 'grandmother' who rattles out stories – and other theatrical entertainment for kids from 12.00 to 14.00 on Sundays. Unfortunately, it's in Lithuanian only, but it might provide some distraction for the kids while you have a meal.

Another family-friendly restaurant is **Marceliukės Klėtis** (🌐 Tuskulėnų 35 📞 5272 5087 🕐 11.00–24.00 Fri & Sat, 11.00–23.00 Sun–Thur), located amid car parks and flats adjacent to Kalvarijų Market – see the northeast corner of the map on page 93. It's a short taxi ride, but you can also get trolleybus 5 or 6 from outside the Novotel hotel. Upstairs is a dining room surrounded by a miniature adventure playground, with a cubby house to explore, lots of mysterious passageways and stairways, and a big slide made from what looks like a fallen log. There's even a low table with child-sized seats, in case they do actually want to sit down and eat. For family-friendly fun, this place is highly recommended, and it's also a decent place to try traditional Lithuanian food.

COMMUNICATIONS

Internet

Most of the Old Town is covered by pay-as-you-go Wi-Fi. You can wander into most cafés and restaurants in the main tourist areas with a laptop and expect to be connected. Some cafés and restaurants offer free Wi-Fi. In both cases, the signal strength and connection speeds are usually excellent.

If you don't have your own computer, you can get on the Internet for free at Cozy (see page 78), where they will happily let you sip and surf using the computer at the bar. There are a few Internet cafés scattered about the city but the best is **Collegium** (❷ Pilies 22), entered through an archway on the left-hand side of a little courtyard.

Phone
Public telephones operate on a card system. You can pick up cards from post offices and kiosks marked 'Lietuvos Spauda'. Paying for the call is the easy part. Working out Lithuania's baffling array of prefixes is the hurdle.

TELEPHONING VILNIUS
The country code for Lithuania is 370 and the area code for Vilnius is 5. Basic telephone numbers have seven digits. If you see a seven-digit Vilnius phone number, you can call it from abroad by dialling 00 370 5 followed by the number.

Note that every phone number in Lithuania is prefixed with an 8 – but only if you're dialling from a mobile phone or from a different city within Lithuania and are not using the international format. To dial Vilnius from Kaunas, for instance, you would dial 8, then 5, then the seven-digit number. To be safe, simply use the international format for all calls you make.

TELEPHONING ABROAD
To make an international call from within Lithuania, dial 00 followed by the country code for the destination country, such as 44 for the UK, 1 for the US and Canada or 61 for Australia. This is followed by the area code (usually omitting the first '0' if there is one) and the number you require.

If you need help using the phones, contact the national telephone company **TEO** (📞 117 from within Vilnius, or 📞 370 8000 0117 from elsewhere 🌐 www.teo.lt).

Post

The postal service in Lithuania is generally very good, although service can be rather abrupt in post offices, where queuing systems for different services are strict and waits can be long. Mail can go missing, so if you want to be sure your letter will arrive, use the registered postal service. Standard rates for postcards are 1.55Lt within Lithuania, 2.45Lt within the EU and 2.90Lt outside the EU but be aware that letters tend to weigh and cost more. See 🌐 www.post.lt for more detailed information.

ELECTRICITY

Lithuania runs on 240 volts using European-style two-pin sockets. Buy adaptors before you come as they are not readily available in the main tourist areas. If you do need to buy an adaptor, head for the Akropolis shopping centre (see page 96) where you will find an 'Elektromarkt' store.

TRAVELLERS WITH DISABILITIES

Vilnius wasn't designed for wheelchair users or people with other disabilities but the city is making efforts to better the situation and things are improving rapidly. There are now plenty of wheelchair-friendly venues but the trouble rests in getting there. The cobbled streets, narrow pavements and abundance of stairs make it difficult for those with wheelchairs or mobility difficulties to get around.

The newer buses and trolleybuses now have low-entry doors and space inside for wheelchairs. These are gradually replacing

△ *A footbridge crosses the river and leads to modern Vilnius*

the older fleet of groaning and lumbering vehicles, which are not recommended for their ease of access. For specific, up-to-date information and advice, contact the **Lithuanian Council for Disabled Affairs** (ⓐ Vivulskio 13 ⓣ 5231 6649).

TOURIST INFORMATION

Tourist information offices are located at:

Central ⓐ Vilniaus 22 ⓣ 5262 9660

Town Hall ⓐ Didžioji 31 ⓣ 5262 6470

Railway station ⓐ Geležinkelio 16 ⓣ 5269 2091

Their website (ⓦ www.turizmas.vilnius.lt) is not always up to date but the staff at the tourist information offices are generally multilingual, pleasant and helpful.

Those visiting Vilnius with an interest in Jewish history and culture should drop into the **Jewish Community Centre** (ⓐ Pylimo 4 ⓣ 5261 3003) or the new **Jewish Cultural and Information Centre** (ⓐ Mėsinių 3a/5 ⓣ 5261 6422).

BACKGROUND READING

Vilnius In Your Pocket is published every four months and is good for up-to-date listings information and reviews. Find it in bookshops, tourist information offices and kiosks.

Vilnius City Guide by Tomas Venclova provides an excellent overview of the city and its history, in a format that is small enough to stick in your bag and carry around as you explore.

Literary books and novels by Lithuanian authors are rarely available in English translation.

Emergencies

112 is the all-purpose emergency number. It works from any fixed or mobile phone in Lithuania. It should be used for all and any genuine emergencies, including police, ambulance and fire. Lithuania does not have a system in place to locate the source of your call, so be prepared to give address details.

Emergencies of the 'chocolate and flowers at midnight' variety are best dealt with by calling the **general information hotline** (☎ 118 or 1588), for which you will pay a small fee.

If you break down while driving anywhere in Lithuania, call **Altas Assistance** (☎ 5240 2380). In Vilnius, they have a basic 35Lt call-out fee plus the cost of any work done. Out of town, expect to pay 75Lt for the call-out.

MEDICAL SERVICES

The main public hospital is the **Vilnius University Emergency Hospital** (@ Šiltnamių 29 ☎ 5216 9212).

There are several private hospitals with English-speaking staff that offer 24-hour emergency care. These include: **Baltic American Medical & Surgical Clinic** (@ Nemenčinės 54a ☎ 5234 2020) and the **Medical Diagnostic Centre** (@ Grybo 32/10 ☎ 5270 9120).

For general medical help during business hours, the most central and convenient option is the **Med General Private Clinic** (@ Gedimino 1a/19, 2nd floor ☎ 6843 3100). Pharmacies (*vaistin*) are plentiful.

For dental help, contact **Air B Mackeviči Odontologijos Klinika** (@ Stuokos-Gucevičiaus 9/9 ☎ 5261 2512).

EMERGENCY PHRASES

Help!	**Fire!**	**Stop!**
Gelbėkit!	Gaisras!	Stop!
Gel-beh-kit!	*Ghays-rus!*	*Stop!*

Call an ambulance/a doctor/ the police/the fire brigade!
Iškvieskite greitàjà pagalbà/gydytojà/policijà/gaisrininkus!
*Ish-ques-kee-teh gray-tah-yah pah-gull-bah/ghee-dee-toh-yah/
poh-lee-tsee-yah/ghay-sree-neen-coos!*

POLICE

The main police station (🄰 Saltoniškių 19, room 107) is located some
way out of the city centre. However, this is just an administrative
office and it is unlikely that anyone there would speak English.

If you need assistance from the police, you should always call
them by telephone using the emergency number 🕿 112

EMBASSIES & CONSULATES

Australia 🄰 Vilniaus 23 🕿 5212 3369
Canada 🄰 Jogailos 4 🕿 5249 0950
Republic of Ireland 🄰 Gedimino 1 🕿 5262 9460
UK 🄰 Antakalnio 2 🕿 5246 2900
USA 🄰 Akmenų 6 🕿 5266 5500

ACKNOWLEDGEMENTS

Thomas Cook Publishing wishes to thank the photographers, picture libraries and other organisations, to whom the copyright belongs, for the photographs in this book.

Dreamstime.com (Aleksak, page 11; Anitabonita, page 61; Atsa, page 66; Birute, page 29; Grauzikas, page 51; Hauhu, page 23; Marc Johnson, page 139; Lukasztyms, page 7; Asta Plechavičiūtė, page 5; Regimantas Ramanauskas, pages 42–3 & 152); elianadulins/iStockphoto.com, pages 47 & 73; Druskininkai Tourist Information, pages 113 & 118; Klaipėda City Municipality, page 115; Andrew Quested, pages 9, 15, 19, 22, 26, 35, 37, 49, 58, 68, 71, 78, 84, 87, 88, 97, 105, 107, 127, 133, 134 & 141; Richard Schofield, pages 98, 121, 123, 128 & 148; SXC.hu (Robert J, page 101; Domantas Jankauskas, page 108); Tourism Division of Vilnius City Municipal Government, pages 12, 21, 25, 45, 65, 94, 111, 117, 145 & 147; Ray Vysniauskas, pages 33 & 38.

Project editor: Jennifer Jahn
Layout: Paul Queripel
Proofreaders: Karolin Thomas & Kelly Walker

Send your thoughts to
books@thomascook.com

- Found a great bar, club, shop or must-see sight that we don't feature?

- Like to tip us off about any information that needs a little updating?

- Want to tell us what you love about this handy little guidebook and more importantly how we can make it even handier?

Then here's your chance to tell all! Send us ideas, discoveries and recommendations today and then look out for your valuable input in the next edition of this title.

Email the above address (stating the title) or write to:
pocket guides Series Editor, Thomas Cook Publishing, PO Box 227, Coningsby Road, Peterborough PE3 8SB, UK.

WHAT'S IN YOUR GUIDEBOOK?

Independent authors Impartial up-to-date information from our travel experts who meticulously source local knowledge.

Experience Thomas Cook's 165 years in the travel industry and guidebook publishing enriches every word with expertise you can trust.

Travel know-how Thomas Cook has thousands of staff working around the globe, all living and breathing travel.

Editors Travel-publishing professionals, pulling everything together to craft a perfect blend of words, pictures, maps and design.

You, the traveller We deliver a practical, no-nonsense approach to information, geared to how you really use it.

Useful phrases

English	Lithuanian	Approx pronunciation

BASICS

English	Lithuanian	Approx pronunciation
Yes	Taip	Teip
No	Ne	Nya
Please	Prašau	Pra-show
Thank you	Ačiū	Ah-choo
Hello	Labas	Lah-bahs
Goodbye	Viso gero	Vee-soh geh-roh
Excuse me/Sorry	Atsiprašau	Aht-see-prah-show
That's OK	Viskas gerai	Vees-kahs geh-ray
I don't speak Lithuanian	Aš nekalbu lietuviškai	Ash nya-kahl-boo lye-too-vish-kay
Do you speak English?	Ar kalbate angliškai?	Ah kahl-bah-teh angle-ish-kay?
Good morning	Labas rytas	Lah-bas ree-tas
Good afternoon	Laba diena	La-bah dye-nah
Good evening	Labas vakaras	Lah-bas vah-car-us
Good night	Labanakt	Lah-bah-nuct
My name is ...	Mano vardas ...	Mah-noh vahr-dahs ...

NUMBERS

English	Lithuanian	Approx pronunciation
One	Vienas	Wienn-us
Two	Du	Doo
Three	Trys	Trees
Four	Keturi	Keh-too-ree
Five	Penki	Pyan-kee
Six	Šeši	Shya-shee
Seven	Septyni	Sep-tee-nee
Eight	Aštuoni	Ash-too-nee
Nine	Devyni	Deh-wee-nee
Ten	Dešimt	Dya-shimt
Twenty	Dvidešimt	Dwee-deh-shimt
Fifty	Penkiasdešimt	Penck-yas-dya-shimt
One hundred	Šimtas	Shim-tahs

SIGNS & NOTICES

English	Lithuanian	Approx pronunciation
Airport	Oro uostas	Oh-roh ohs-tahs
Railway station	Geležinkelio stotis	Girl-ezh-ink-ello stoh-tiss
Platform	Platforma	Plat-form-ah
Smoking/ non-smoking	Rūkoma/ nerūkoma	Roo-koh-mah/ nya-roo-koh-mah
Toilets	Tualetas	Too-al-ett-us
Ladies/Gentlemen	Moterų/Vyrų	Mot-err-oo/Weer-oo
Underground	Metro	Met-roh